THE UK TOWER
FRYER COOKBOOK
FOR BEGINNERS

365 Days Quick&Easy, affordable and Vibrant Air Fryer Homemade Recipes Anyone

Can Make At Home

SALENA L. MELENDEZ

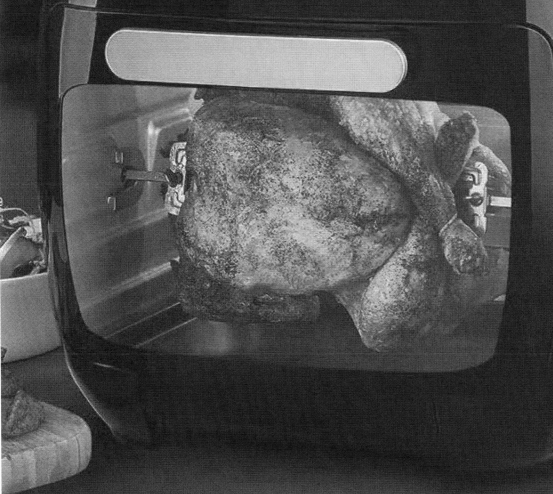

Table of Contents

The UK Tower Air Fryer is an excellent appliance for enjoying healthy meals. A major issue with deep-frying is that it uses an incredibly copious amount of oil, which is not good for your health. You can eliminate almost all oil from your meals with an air fryer.

Having acquired your first air fryer, the issue is what you can cook with it. You may not have made the decision yet on whether to buy one or not. Your hesitancy may be based on the false belief that it is only good for making French fries. However, the recipes below easily debunk that. An air fryer is a highly versatile piece of cooking equipment that could replace many kitchen appliances. An all-in-one appliance that brings convenience, speed, and healthy cooking. With the right recipes and guidance, you can prepare almost any meal and enjoy the most diverse flavors from the comfort of your kitchen.

Once you acquire an air fryer, its convenience and ease of use probably mean you will use it daily. The only limitation is that the typical air fryer comes with a single compartment. Once you get into it, most people acquire a second air fryer so they can easily prepare entire meals.

I have personally been in the privileged position of reviewing numerous air fryers and using them. It has given me the opportunity to understand all the hype, and I am confident it is not hype. Air fryers can be used to prepare almost any meal you can imagine.

Chapter 1
Basics of The UK Tower Air Fryer

Some cookbooks are so dull because of how complex they can be. The result is that most people need more time to come up with complex meals. As a result, most people with a cookbook only use it once a month or during a special event when they have some free time.

With an air fryer, you can enjoy delicious meals at your convenience. It takes a small amount of time and energy to prepare the meals. Once they are in the air fryer, you only have to press a few buttons and sit back as the appliance does the rest.

The UK Tower air fryer is convenient for cooking all types of meals. You can make your favorite meat dishes, vegetables, pastries, and more. The only limit is your imagination.

How Does The UK Tower Air Fryer Technology Work

Tower Air Fryers using an invention called Vortx Technology. It has revolutionized the cooking process for people all over the world. The technology improves efficiency over all other cooking methods.

Another benefit of the technology is that it speeds up the cooking while eliminating unevenness in cooked meals. With traditional pots and pans, most meals will have unevenness, no matter how much care one takes. Vortx technology works by circulating hot air via a heating matric. By covering food with hot air, the air fryer ensures that meals are evenly cooked to a fine crisp each time without having to use oil.

The Process of Cooking with a UK Tower Air Fryer

To cook meals, the top section of the air fryer contains a heating mechanism that superheats air. The food is placed in a basket; once it is turned on, hot air rushes into it. The result is crisp food that feels deep-fried without excessive oil. To cook with an air fryer, below is the simple three-step process you will use:

PLACE FOOD IN A BASKET
An air fryer features a deep-frying style basket where you place your food. The size will vary depending on the air fryer that you use. For some meals, you need to add about a teaspoon of oil to make the food crispy. You can add foil to make the cleanup process faster.

SET THE TIMER
Once you close the air fryer, set your time and temperature, which can be anything from five minutes to half an hour at a temperature of 350 F to 400F. The setting will depend on what you are cooking and how well done you want it.

LET IT COOK

For most meals, you need to sit back and let it cook. However, you might need to flip the meals halfway through the process to ensure it is cooked to an even crisp. Once you are done cooking, ensure that you clean the air fryer, this will ensure cooking the next meal is as easy as possible.

What Can You Cook with an Air Fryer?

Many people imagine an air fryer is only good for meals that would normally be deep-fried. However, it can be used for many other types of meals. These include:

FROZEN FINGER FOOD

An air fryer can prepare things like mozzarella sticks, frozen French fries, and chicken nuggets.

HOMEMADE FINGER FOOD

You can air fry homemade finger food as well. For instance, air-fryer sweet potato fries, potato chips, and other homemade snacks can be made in an air fryer. Even things as diverse as egg rolls can be made in the air fryer. However, you can not place something like fresh cheese there, as it will become a gooey mess.

DIFFERENT MEATS

You can cook chicken, beef, pork, and other meats into a tender and juicy consistency with an air fryer. The air fryer is an excellent choice if you want healthier key meatballs. It also works great for seafood and fish.

VEGETABLES

An air fryer is your best friend if you would love to enjoy roasted vegetables without all the oil. It is an especially convenient option when cooking small meals for one or two people.

BAKED GOODS

You can prepare baked goods in an air fryer such as cookies and apple fritters. You can also try lava cakes in the air fryer and mini doughnut holes. Additionally, you can use the air fryer to prepare breakfast meals such as bacon cinnamon rolls and French toast sticks.

However, it will not work for something that uses liquid batter, uncles; it has to be frozen first.

Find Recipes that Work for You
If you are still trying to decide what to make with your air fryer, the below recipes are for you. They are creative, delicious, and easy to make. You can pick a recipe daily with your UK Tower Air Fryer.

Chapter 2
Staples

Milky Corn Meal

Prep time: 3 minutes | Cook time: 1 hour 5 minutes | Makes about 4 cups

- 1 cup corn meal or polenta (not instant or quick cook)
- 2 cups chicken or vegetable stock
- 2 cups milk
- 2 tablespoons unsalted butter, cut into 4 pieces
- 1 teaspoon flake salt or ½ teaspoon fine salt

1. Add the corn meal to a baking pan. Stir in the stock, milk, butter, and salt.
2. Press the Power Button. Cook at 160°C for 1 hour and 5 minutes.
3. After 15 minutes, remove from the air fryer oven and stir the polenta. Return to the air fryer oven and continue cooking.
4. After 30 minutes, remove the pan again and stir the polenta again. Return to the air fryer oven and continue cooking for 15 to 20 minutes, or until the polenta is soft and creamy and the liquid is absorbed.
5. When done, remove from the air fryer oven.
6. Serve immediately.

Baked Rice

Prep time: 3 minutes | Cook time: 35 minutes | Makes about 4 cups

- 1 cup long-grain white rice, rinsed and drained
- 1 tablespoon unsalted butter, melted, or 1 tablespoon extra-virgin olive oil
- 2 cups water
- 1 teaspoon flake salt or ½ teaspoon fine salt

1. Add the butter and rice to a baking pan and stir to coat. Pour in the water and sprinkle with the salt. Stir until the salt is dissolved.
2. Press the Power Button. Cook at 160°C for 35 minutes.
3. After 20 minutes, remove from the air fryer oven. Stir the rice. Transfer the pan back to the air fryer oven and continue cooking for 10 to 15 minutes, or until the rice is mostly cooked through and the water is absorbed.
4. When done, remove from the air fryer oven and cover with tin foil . Let stand for 10 minutes. Using a fork, gently fluff the rice.
5. Serve immediately.

Asian Dipping Sauce

Prep time: 15 minutes | Cook time: 0 minutes | Makes about 1 cup

- ¼ cup rice vinegar
- ¼ cup hoisin sauce
- ¼ cup low-sodium chicken or vegetable stock
- 3 tablespoons soy sauce
- 1 tablespoon minced or grated ginger
- 1 tablespoon minced or pressed garlic
- 1 teaspoon chili-garlic sauce or sriracha (or more to taste)

1. Stir together all the ingredients in a small bowl, or place in a jar with a tight-fitting lid and shake until well mixed.
2. Use immediately.

Caesar Salad Dressing

Prep time: 5 minutes | Cook time: 0 minutes | Makes about ⅔ cup

- ½ cup extra-virgin olive oil
- 2 tablespoons freshly squeezed lemon juice
- 1 teaspoon anchovy paste
- ¼ teaspoon flake salt or ⅛ teaspoon fine salt
- ¼ teaspoon minced or pressed garlic
- 1 egg, beaten

1. Add all the ingredients to a tall, narrow container.
2. Purée the mixture with an immersion blender until smooth.
3. Use immediately.

Classic Marinara Sauce

Prep time: 15 minutes | Cook time: 30 minutes | Makes about 3 cups

- ¼ cup extra-virgin olive oil
- 3 garlic cloves, minced
- 1 small onion, chopped (about ½ cup)
- 2 tablespoons minced or puréed sun-dried tomatoes (optional)
- 1 (28-ounce / 794-g) can crushed tomatoes
- ½ teaspoon dried basil
- ½ teaspoon dried oregano
- ¼ teaspoon red pepper flakes
- 1 teaspoon flake salt or ½ teaspoon fine salt, plus more as needed

1. Heat the oil in a medium saucepan over medium heat.
2. Add the garlic and onion and sauté for 2 to 3 minutes, or until the onion is softened. Add the sun-dried tomatoes (if desired) and cook for 1 minute until fragrant. Stir in the crushed tomatoes, scraping any brown bits from the bottom of the pot. Fold in the basil, oregano, red pepper flakes, and salt. Stir well.
3. Bring to a simmer. Cook covered for about 30 minutes, stirring occasionally.
4. Turn off the heat and allow the sauce to cool for about 10 minutes.
5. Taste and adjust the seasoning, adding more salt if needed.
6. Use immediately.

Enchilada Sauce

Prep time: 15 minutes | Cook time: 0 minutes | Makes 2 cups

- 3 large ancho chiles, stems and seeds removed, torn into pieces
- 1½ cups very hot water
- 2 garlic cloves, peeled and lightly smashed
- 2 tablespoons wine vinegar
- 1½ teaspoons sugar
- ½ teaspoon dried oregano
- ½ teaspoon ground cumin
- 2 teaspoons flake salt or 1 teaspoon fine salt

1. Mix together the chile pieces and hot water in a bowl and let stand for 10 to 15 minutes.
2. Pour the chiles and water into a blender jar. Fold in the garlic, vinegar, sugar, oregano, cumin, and salt and blend until smooth.
3. Use immediately.

Roasted Mushrooms

Prep time: 8 minutes | Cook time: 30 minutes | Makes about 1½ cups

- 1 pound (454 g) button or cremini mushrooms, washed, stems trimmed, and cut into quarters or thick slices
- ¼ cup water
- 1 teaspoon flake salt or ½ teaspoon fine salt
- 3 tablespoons unsalted butter, cut into pieces, or extra-virgin olive oil

1. Place a large piece of tin foil on a sheet pan. Place the mushroom pieces in the middle of the foil. Spread them out into an even layer. Pour the water over them, season with the salt, and add the butter. Wrap the mushrooms in the foil.
2. Press the Power Button. Cook at 160°C for 15 minutes.
3. After 15 minutes, remove from the air fryer oven. Transfer the foil packet to a cutting board and carefully unwrap it. Pour the mushrooms and cooking liquid from the foil onto the sheet pan.
4. Return the pan to the air fryer oven. Press the Power Button. Cook at 180°C for 15 minutes.
5. After about 10 minutes, remove from the air fryer oven and stir the mushrooms. Return to the air fryer oven and continue cooking for anywhere from 5 to 15 more minutes, or until the liquid is mostly gone and the mushrooms start to brown.
6. Serve immediately.

Shawarma Spice Mix

Prep time: 5 minutes | Cook time: 0 minutes | Makes about 1 tablespoon

- 1 teaspoon smoked paprika
- 1 teaspoon cumin
- ¼ teaspoon turmeric
- ¼ teaspoon flake salt or ⅛ teaspoon fine salt
- ¼ teaspoon cinnamon
- ¼ teaspoon allspice
- ¼ teaspoon red pepper flakes
- ¼ teaspoon freshly ground black pepper

1. Stir together all the ingredients in a small bowl.
2. Use immediately or place in an airtight container in the pantry.

Simple Teriyaki Sauce

Prep time: 5 minutes | Cook time: 0 minutes | Makes ¾ cup

- ½ cup soy sauce
- 3 tablespoons honey
- 1 tablespoon rice wine or dry sherry
- 1 tablespoon rice vinegar
- 2 teaspoons minced fresh ginger
- 2 garlic cloves, smashed

1. Beat together all the ingredients in a small bowl.
2. Use immediately.

Polenta with Butter

Prep time: 3 minutes | Cook time: 1 hour 5 minutes | Makes about 4 cups

- 1 cup corn meal or polenta (not instant or quick cook)
- 2 cups chicken or vegetable stock
- 2 cups milk
- 2 tablespoons unsalted butter, cut into 4 pieces
- 1 teaspoon flake salt or ½ teaspoon fine salt

1. Add the corn meal to the baking pan. Stir in the stock, milk, butter, and salt.
2. Select Bake, set the temperature to 160°C, and set the time for 1 hour and 5 minutes. Select Start/Stop to begin preheating.
3. Once the unit has preheated, place the pan on the bake position.
4. After 15 minutes, remove the pan from the oven and stir the polenta. Return the pan to the oven and continue cooking.
5. After 30 minutes, remove the pan again and stir the polenta again. Return the pan to the oven and continue cooking for 15 to 20 minutes, or until the polenta is soft and creamy and the liquid is absorbed.
6. When done, remove the pan from the oven.
7. Serve immediately.

Spice Mix with Cumin

Prep time: 5 minutes | Cook time: 0 minutes | Makes about 1 tablespoon

- 1 teaspoon smoked paprika
- 1 teaspoon cumin
- ¼ teaspoon turmeric
- ¼ teaspoon flake salt or ⅛ teaspoon fine salt
- ¼ teaspoon cinnamon
- ¼ teaspoon allspice
- ¼ teaspoon red pepper flakes
- ¼ teaspoon freshly ground black pepper

1. Stir together all the ingredients in a small bowl.
2. Use immediately or place in an airtight container in the pantry.

Chile Seasoning

Prep time: 5 minutes | Cook time: 0 minutes | Makes about ¼ cups

- 3 tablespoons ancho chile powder
- 3 tablespoons paprika
- 2 tablespoons dried oregano
- 2 tablespoons freshly ground black pepper
- 2 teaspoons cayenne
- 2 teaspoons cumin
- 1 tablespoon granulated onion
- 1 tablespoon granulated garlic

1. Stir together all the ingredients in a small bowl.
2. Use immediately or place in an airtight container in the pantry.

Chapter 3
Breakfast

Breakfast Cheddar Calzone

Prep time: 15 minutes | Cook time: 15 minutes | Serves 4

- 1½ cups shredded Mozzarella cheese
- ½ cup blanched finely ground almond flour
- 1 ounce (28 g) full-fat cream cheese
- 1 large whole egg
- 4 large eggs, scrambled
- ½ pound (227 g) cooked breakfast banger, crumbled
- 8 tablespoons shredded mild Cheddar cheese

1. In a large microwave-safe bowl, add Mozzarella, almond flour, and cream cheese. Microwave for 1 minute. Stir until the mixture is smooth and forms a ball. Add the egg and stir until dough forms.
2. Place dough between two sheets of parchment and roll out to ¼-inch thickness. Cut the dough into four rectangles.
3. Mix scrambled eggs and cooked banger together in a large bowl. Divide the mixture evenly among each piece of dough, placing it on the lower half of the rectangle. Sprinkle each with 2 tablespoons Cheddar.
4. Fold over the rectangle to cover the egg and meat mixture. Pinch, roll, or use a wet fork to close the edges completely.
5. Cut a piece of parchment to fit your air fryer basket or wire rack and place the calzones onto the parchment. Place parchment into the air fryer basket or wire rack.
6. Adjust the temperature to 190°C and air fry for 15 minutes.
7. Flip the calzones halfway through the cooking time. When done, calzones should be golden in colour. Serve immediately.

Pork banger and Cheese Balls

Prep time: 10 minutes | Cook time: 12 minutes | Makes 16 balls

- 1 pound (454 g) pork breakfast banger
- ½ cup shredded Cheddar cheese
- 1 ounce (28 g) full-fat cream cheese, softened
- 1 large egg

1. Mix all ingredients in a large bowl. Form into sixteen (1-inch) balls. Place the balls into the air fryer basket or wire rack.
2. Adjust the temperature to 200°C and air fry for 12 minutes.
3. Shake the air fryer basket or wire rack two or three times during cooking. banger balls will be browned on the outside and have an internal temperature of at least 60°C when completely cooked.
4. Serve warm.

Mexican-Style Shakshuka

Prep time: 5 minutes | Cook time: 6 minutes | Serves 1

- ½ cup salsa
- 2 large eggs, room temperature
- ½ teaspoon fine sea salt
- ¼ teaspoon smoked paprika
- ⅛ teaspoon ground cumin

FOR GARNISH:

- 2 tablespoons Coriander leaves

1. Preheat the air fryer to 200°C.
2. Place the salsa in a pie pan or a casserole dish that will fit into your air fryer. Crack the eggs into the salsa and sprinkle them with the salt, paprika, and cumin.
3. Place the pan in the air fryer and bake for 6 minutes, or until the egg whites are set and the yolks are cooked to your liking.
4. Remove from the air fryer and garnish with the Coriander before serving.
5. Best served fresh.

Mini Cinnamon Biscuits

Prep time: 15 minutes | Cook time: 13 minutes | Makes 8 biscuits

- 2 cups blanched almond flour
- ½ cup Swerve confectioners'-style sweetener or equivalent amount of liquid or powdered sweetener
- 1 teaspoon baking powder
- ½ teaspoon fine sea salt
- ¼ cup plus 2 tablespoons (¾ stick) very cold unsalted butter
- ¼ cup unsweetened, unflavoured almond milk
- 1 large egg
- 1 teaspoon vanilla extract
- 3 teaspoons ground cinnamon
- Glaze:
- ½ cup Swerve confectioners'-style sweetener or equivalent amount of powdered sweetener
- ¼ cup double cream or unsweetened, unflavoured almond milk

1. Preheat the air fryer to 180°C. Line a pie pan that fits into your air fryer with greaseproof paper.
2. In a medium-sized bowl, mix together the almond flour, sweetener (if powdered; do not add liquid sweetener), baking powder, and salt. Cut the butter into ½-inch squares, then use a hand mixer to work the butter into the dry ingredients. When you are done, the mixture should still have chunks of butter.
3. In a small bowl, whisk together the almond milk, egg, and vanilla extract (if using liquid sweetener, add it as well) until blended. Using a fork, stir the wet ingredients into the dry ingredients until large clumps form. Add the cinnamon and use your hands to swirl it into the dough.
4. Form the dough into sixteen 1-inch balls and place them on the prepared pan, spacing them about ½ inch apart. (If you're using a smaller air fryer, work in batches if necessary.) Bake in the air fryer until golden, 10 to 13 minutes. Remove from the air fryer and let cool on the pan for at least 5 minutes.
5. While the biscuits bake, make the glaze: Place the powdered sweetener in a small bowl and slowly stir in the double cream with a fork.
6. When the biscuits have cooled somewhat, dip the tops into the glaze, allow it to dry a bit, and then dip again for a thick glaze.
7. Serve warm or at room temperature. Store unglazed biscuits in an airtight container in the refrigerator for up to 3 days or in the freezer for up to a month. Reheat in a preheated 180°C air fryer for 5 minutes, or until warmed through, and dip in the glaze as instructed above.

Air-Fried Meritage Eggs
Prep time: 5 minutes | Cook time: 8 minutes | Serves 2

- 2 teaspoons unsalted butter (or coconut oil for dairy-free), for greasing the ramekins
- 4 large eggs
- 2 teaspoons chopped fresh thyme
- ½ teaspoon fine sea salt
- ¼ teaspoon ground black pepper
- 2 tablespoons double cream (or unsweetened, unflavoured almond milk for dairy-free)
- 3 tablespoons finely grated Parmesan cheese (or Kite Hill brand chive cream cheese style spread, softened, for dairy-free)
- Fresh thyme leaves, for garnish (optional)

1. Preheat the air fryer to 200°C. Grease two (4-ounce / 113-g) ramekins with the butter.
2. Crack 2 eggs into each ramekin and divide the thyme, salt, and pepper between the ramekins. Pour 1 tablespoon of the double cream into each ramekin. Sprinkle each ramekin with 1½ tablespoons of the Parmesan cheese.
3. Place the ramekins in the air fryer and bake for 8 minutes for soft-cooked yolks (longer if you desire a harder yolk).
4. Garnish with a sprinkle of ground black pepper and thyme leaves, if desired. Best served fresh.

Breakfast Pepperoni Pizza
Prep time: 5 minutes | Cook time: 8 minutes | Serves 1

- 2 large eggs
- ¼ cup unsweetened, unflavoured almond milk (or unflavoured hemp milk for nut-free)
- ¼ teaspoon fine sea salt
- ⅛ teaspoon ground black pepper
- ¼ cup diced onions
- ¼ cup shredded Parmesan cheese (omit for dairy-free)
- 6 pepperoni slices (omit for vegetarian)
- ¼ teaspoon dried oregano leaves
- ¼ cup pizza sauce, warmed, for serving

1. Preheat the air fryer to 180°C. Grease a cake pan.
2. In a small bowl, use a fork to whisk together the eggs, almond milk, salt, and pepper. Add the onions and stir to mix. Pour the mixture into the greased pan. Top with the cheese (if using), pepperoni slices (if using), and oregano.
3. Place the pan in the air fryer and bake for 8 minutes, or until the eggs are cooked to your liking.
4. Loosen the eggs from the sides of the pan with a spatula and place them on a serving plate. Drizzle the pizza sauce on top. Best served fresh.

Denver Ham Omelet

Prep time: 5 minutes | Cook time: 8 minutes | Serves 1

- 2 large eggs
- ¼ cup unsweetened, unflavoured almond milk
- ¼ teaspoon fine sea salt
- ⅛ teaspoon ground black pepper
- ¼ cup diced ham (omit for vegetarian)
- ¼ cup diced green and red bell peppers
- 2 tablespoons diced spring onions, plus more for garnish
- ¼ cup shredded Cheddar cheese (about 1 ounce / 28 g) (omit for dairy-free)
- Quartered cherry tomatoes, for serving (optional)

1. Preheat the air fryer to 180°C. Grease a cake pan and set aside.
2. In a small bowl, use a fork to whisk together the eggs, almond milk, salt, and pepper. Add the ham, bell peppers, and spring onions. Pour the mixture into the greased pan. Add the cheese on top (if using).
3. Place the pan in the air fryer basket or wire rack of the air fryer. Bake for 8 minutes, or until the eggs are cooked to your liking.
4. Loosen the omelet from the sides of the pan with a spatula and place it on a serving plate. Garnish with spring onions and serve with cherry tomatoes, if desired. Best served fresh.

Ritzy Breakfast Sammies

Prep time: 15 minutes | Cook time: 20 minutes | Serves 5

BISCUITS:

- 6 large egg whites
- 2 cups blanched almond flour, plus more if needed
- 1½ teaspoons baking powder
- ½ teaspoon fine sea salt
- ¼ cup (½ stick) very cold unsalted butter (or lard for dairy-free), cut into ¼-inch pieces

EGGS:

- 5 large eggs
- ½ teaspoon fine sea salt
- ¼ teaspoon ground black pepper
- 5 (1-ounce / 28-g) slices Cheddar cheese (omit for dairy-free)
- 10 thin slices ham

1. Spray the air fryer basket or wire rack with avocado oil. Preheat the air fryer to 180°C. Grease two pie pans or two baking pans that will fit inside your air fryer.
2. Make the biscuits: In a medium-sized bowl, whip the egg whites with a hand mixer until very stiff. Set aside.
3. In a separate medium-sized bowl, stir together the almond flour, baking powder, and salt until well combined. Cut in the butter. Gently fold the flour mixture into the egg whites with a rubber spatula. If the dough is too wet to form into mounds, add a few tablespoons of almond flour until the dough holds together well.
4. Using a large spoon, divide the dough into 5 equal portions and drop them about 1 inch apart on one of the greased pie pans. (If you're using a smaller air fryer, work in batches if necessary.) Place the pan in the air fryer and bake for 11 to 14 minutes, until the biscuits are golden brown. Remove from the air fryer and set aside to cool.
5. Make the eggs: Set the air fryer to 190°C. Crack the eggs into the remaining greased pie pan and sprinkle with the salt and pepper. Place the eggs in the air fryer to bake for 5 minutes, or until they are cooked to your liking.
6. Open the air fryer and top each egg yolk with a slice of cheese (if using). Bake for another minute, or until the cheese is melted.
7. Once the biscuits are cool, slice them in half lengthwise. Place 1 cooked egg topped with cheese and 2 slices of ham in each biscuit.
8. Store leftover biscuits, eggs, and ham in separate airtight containers in the fridge for up to 3 days. Reheat the biscuits and eggs on a baking tray in a preheated 180°C air fryer for 5 minutes, or until warmed through.

kebab Breakfast Patties with Tzatziki Sauce

Prep time: 10 minutes | Cook time: 20 minutes per batch | Makes 16 patties

PATTIES:

- 2 pounds (907 g) ground lamb or beef
- ½ cup diced red onions
- ¼ cup sliced black olives
- 2 tablespoons tomato sauce
- 1 teaspoon dried oregano leaves
- 1 teaspoon Greek seasoning
- 2 cloves garlic, minced
- 1 teaspoon fine sea salt

TZATZIKI:

- 1 cup full-fat Soured cream
- 1 small cucumber, chopped
- ½ teaspoon fine sea salt
- ½ teaspoon garlic powder, or 1 clove garlic, minced
- ¼ teaspoon dried dill weed, or 1 teaspoon finely chopped fresh dill
- For Garnish/Serving:
- ½ cup crumbled feta cheese (about 2 ounces / 57 g)
- Diced red onions
- Sliced black olives
- Sliced cucumbers

1. Preheat the air fryer to 180°C.
2. Place the ground lamb, onions, olives, tomato sauce, oregano, Greek seasoning, garlic, and salt in a large bowl. Mix well to combine the ingredients.
3. Using your hands, form the mixture into sixteen 3-inch patties. Place about 5 of the patties in the air fryer and air fry for 20 minutes, flipping halfway through. Remove the patties and place them on a serving platter. Repeat with the remaining patties.
4. While the patties cook, make the tzatziki: Place all the ingredients in a small bowl and stir well. Cover and store in the fridge until ready to serve. Garnish with ground black pepper before serving.
5. Serve the patties with a dollop of tzatziki, a sprinkle of crumbled feta cheese, diced red onions, sliced black olives, and sliced cucumbers.
6. Store leftovers in an airtight container in the refrigerator for up to 5 days or in the freezer for up to a month. Reheat the patties in a preheated 200°C air fryer for a few minutes, until warmed through.

Quiche Bake

Prep time: 10 minutes | Cook time: 1 hour | Makes 1 (6-inch) quiche

CRUST:

- 1¼ cups blanched almond flour
- 1¼ cups grated Parmesan or Gouda cheese
- ¼ teaspoon fine sea salt
- 1 large egg, beaten

FILLING:

- ½ cup chicken or beef broth (or vegetable broth for vegetarian)
- 1 cup shredded Emmethaler (about 4 ounces / 113 g)
- 4 ounces (113 g) cream cheese (½ cup)
- 1 tablespoon unsalted butter, melted
- 4 large eggs, beaten
- ⅓ cup minced leeks or sliced spring onions
- ¾ teaspoon fine sea salt
- ⅛ teaspoon cayenne pepper
- Chopped spring onions, for garnish

1. Preheat the air fryer to 160°C. Grease a pie pan. Spray two large pieces of greaseproof paper with avocado oil and set them on the countertop.
2. Make the crust: In a medium-sized bowl, combine the flour, cheese, and salt and mix well. Add the egg and mix until the dough is well combined and stiff.
3. Place the dough in the center of one of the greased pieces of parchment. Top with the other piece of parchment. Using a rolling pin, roll out the dough into a circle about 1/16 inch thick.
4. Press the pie crust into the prepared pie pan. Place it in the air fryer and bake for 12 minutes, or until it starts to lightly brown.
5. While the crust bakes, make the filling: In a large bowl, combine the broth, Emmethaler, cream cheese, and butter. Stir in the eggs, leeks, salt, and cayenne pepper. When the crust is ready, pour the mixture into the crust.
6. Place the quiche in the air fryer and bake for 15 minutes. Turn the heat down to 150°C and bake for an additional 30 minutes, or until a knife inserted 1 inch from the edge comes out clean. You may have to cover the edges of the crust with foil to prevent burning.
7. Allow the quiche to cool for 10 minutes before garnishing it with chopped spring onions and cutting it into wedges.
8. Store leftovers in an airtight container in the refrigerator for up to 4 days or in the freezer for up to a month. Reheat in a preheated 180°C air fryer for a few minutes, until warmed through.

Southwest Seasoning

Prep time: 5 minutes | Cook time: 0 minutes | Makes about ¾ cups

- 3 tablespoons ancho chile powder
- 3 tablespoons paprika
- 2 tablespoons dried oregano
- 2 tablespoons freshly ground black pepper
- 2 teaspoons cayenne
- 2 teaspoons cumin
- 1 tablespoon granulated onion
- 1 tablespoon granulated garlic

1. Stir together all the ingredients in a small bowl.
2. Use immediately or place in an airtight container in the pantry.

Parmesan Ranch Onion Risotto

Prep time: 10 minutes | Cook time: 30 minutes | Serves 2

- 1 tablespoon olive oil
- 1 clove garlic, minced
- 1 tablespoon unsalted butter
- 1 onion, diced
- ¾ cup Arborio rice
- 2 cups chicken stock, boiling
- ½ cup Parmesan cheese, grated

1. Preheat the air fryer to 200°C.
2. Grease a round baking tin with olive oil and stir in the garlic, butter, and onion.
3. Transfer the tin to the air fryer and bake for 4 minutes. Add the rice and bake for 4 more minutes.
4. Turn the air fryer to 160°C and pour in the chicken stock. Cover and bake for 22 minutes.
5. Scatter with cheese and serve.

Parmesan Egg and banger Muffins
Prep time: 5 minutes | Cook time: 20 minutes | Serves 4

- 6 ounces (170 g) Italian banger, sliced
- 6 eggs
- ⅛ cup double cream
- Salt and ground black pepper, to taste
- 3 ounces (85 g) Parmesan cheese, grated

1. Preheat the air fryer to 180°C. Grease a muffin pan.
2. Put the sliced banger in the muffin pan.
3. Beat the eggs with the cream in a bowl and season with salt and pepper.
4. Pour half of the mixture over the bangers in the pan.
5. Sprinkle with cheese and the remaining egg mixture.
6. Bake in the preheated air fryer for 20 minutes or until set.
7. Serve immediately.

Mozzarella Pepperoni Pizza
Prep time: 10 minutes | Cook time: 6 minutes | Serves 1

- 1 teaspoon olive oil
- 1 tablespoon pizza sauce
- 1 pita bread
- 6 pepperoni slices
- ¼ cup grated Mozzarella cheese
- ¼ teaspoon garlic powder
- ¼ teaspoon dried oregano

1. Preheat the air fryer to 180°C. Grease the baking pan with olive oil.
2. Spread the pizza sauce on top of the pita bread. Put the pepperoni slices over the sauce, followed by the Mozzarella cheese.
3. Season with garlic powder and oregano.
4. Put the pita pizza inside the air fryer and place a trivet on top.
5. Bake in the preheated air fryer for 6 minutes and serve.

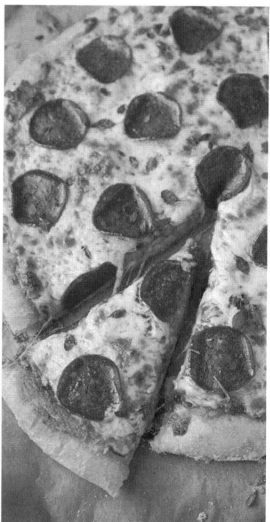

Blueberry Muffins

Prep time: 10 minutes | Cook time: 12 minutes | Makes 8 muffins

- 1⅓ cups flour
- ½ cup sugar
- 2 teaspoons baking powder
- ¼ teaspoon salt
- ⅓ cup rapeseed oil
- 1 egg
- ½ cup milk
- ⅔ cup blueberries, fresh or frozen and thawed

1. Preheat the air fryer to 170°C.
2. In a medium bowl, stir together flour, sugar, baking powder, and salt.
3. In a separate bowl, combine oil, egg, and milk and mix well.
4. Add egg mixture to dry ingredients and stir just until moistened.
5. Gently stir in the blueberries.
6. Spoon batter evenly into greaseproof paper-lined muffin cups.
7. Put 4 muffin cups in the baking pan and bake for 12 minutes or until tops spring back when touched lightly.
8. Repeat previous step to bake remaining muffins.
9. Serve immediately.

Brown Rice Porridge with Coconut and Dates

Prep time: 5 minutes | Cook time: 23 minutes | Serves 1 or 2

- ½ cup cooked brown rice
- 1 cup tinned coconut milk
- ¼ cup unsweetened desiccated coconut
- ¼ cup packed dark Demerara sugar
- 4 large Medjool dates, pitted and roughly chopped
- ½ teaspoon flaked salt
- ¼ teaspoon ground cardamom
- double cream, for serving (optional)

1. Preheat the air fryer to 190°C.
2. Place all the ingredients except the double cream in a baking pan and stir until blended.
3. Transfer the pan to the air fryer and bake for about 23 minutes until the porridge is thick and creamy. Stir the porridge halfway through the cooking time.
4. Remove from the air fryer and ladle the porridge into bowls.
5. Serve hot with a drizzle of the cream, if desired.

Chapter 4
Poultry

Gai Yang Chicken

Prep time: 15 minutes | Cook time: 65 minutes| Serves 4

- 2-pounds Cornish hens, roughly chopped
- 2 tablespoons Gai yang spices
- 1 tablespoon avocado oil

1. Rub the hens with spices carefully.
2. Then sprinkle the hens with avocado oil and put in the air fryer.
3. Cook the meal at 180°C for 65 minutes.

Garlic Chicken Wings

Prep time: 5 minutes | Cook time: 30 minutes | Serves4

- 2 pounds chicken wings
- ¼ cup olive oil
- Juice of 2 lemons
- Zest of 1 lemon, grated
- A pinch of salt and black pepper
- 2 garlic cloves, minced

1. In a bowl, mix the chicken wings with the rest of the ingredients and toss well.
2. Put the chicken wings in your air fryer's basket and cook at 400 degrees F for 30 minutes, shaking halfway.
3. Divide between plates and serve with a side salad.

Provolone Meatballs

Prep time: 10 minutes | Cook time: 12 minutes | Serves 6

- 12 oz ground chicken
- ½ cup coconut flour
- 2 egg whites, whisked
- 1 teaspoon ground black pepper
- 1 egg yolk
- 1 teaspoon salt
- 4 oz Provolone cheese, grated
- 1 teaspoon ground oregano
- ½ teaspoon chili powder
- 1 tablespoon avocado oil

1. In the mixing bowl mix up ground chicken, ground black pepper, egg yolk, salt, Provolone cheese, ground oregano, and chili powder.
2. Stir the mixture until homogenous and make the small meatballs. Dip the meatballs in the whisked egg whites and coat in the coconut flour.
3. Preheat the air fryer to 180°C. Put the chicken meatballs in the air fryer basket or wire rack and cook them for 6 minutes from both sides.

Almond Meatballs

Prep time: 10 minutes | Cook time: 12 minutes| Serves 6

- 16 oz ground chicken
- ½ cup almond flour
- 1 teaspoon salt
- 1 teaspoon ground black pepper
- 1 tablespoon avocado oil

1. Mix ground chicken with almond flour, salt, and ground black pepper.
2. After this, make the meatballs and put them in the air fryer in one layer.
3. Sprinkle the meatballs with avocado oil and cook at 180°C for 12 minutes.

Cream Cheese Chicken Mix

Prep time: 15 minutes | Cook time: 16 minutes | Serves 4

- 1-pound chicken wings
- ¼ cup cream cheese
- 1 tablespoon apple cider vinegar
- 1 teaspoon Truvia
- ½ teaspoon smoked paprika
- ½ teaspoon ground nutmeg
- 1 teaspoon avocado oil

1. In the mixing bowl mix up cream cheese, Truvia, apple cider vinegar, smoked paprika, and ground nutmeg. Then add the chicken wings and coat them in the cream cheese mixture well.
2. Leave the chicken winds in the cream cheese mixture for 10-15 minutes to marinate. Meanwhile, preheat the air fryer to 190°C.
3. Put the chicken wings in the air fryer and cook them for 8 minutes. Then flip the chicken wings on another and brush with cream cheese marinade.
4. Cook the chicken wings for 8 minutes more.

Lemon Chicken Thighs
Prep time: 5 minutes | Cook time: 30 minutes | Serves 4

- 8 chicken thighs, boneless, skinless
- 1 tablespoon lemon zest, grated
- 2 tablespoons lemon juice
- 1 teaspoon avocado oil
- 1 teaspoon salt

1. Rub the chicken thighs with lemon zest, lemon juice, avocado oil, and salt.
2. Put the chicken thighs in the air fryer basket or wire rack and cook at 180°C for 30 minutes.
3. Flip the chicken thighs on another side after 15 minutes of cooking.

Lemon and Chili Chicken Drumsticks
Prep time: 10 minutes | Cook time: 20 minutes | Serves 6

- 6 chicken drumsticks
- 1 teaspoon dried oregano
- 1 tablespoon lemon juice
- ½ teaspoon lemon zest, grated
- 1 teaspoon ground cumin
- ½ teaspoon chili flakes
- 1 teaspoon garlic powder
- ½ teaspoon ground coriander
- 1 tablespoon avocado oil

1. Rub the chicken drumsticks with dried oregano, lemon juice, lemon zest, ground cumin, chili flakes, garlic powder, and ground coriander.
2. Then sprinkle them with avocado oil and put in the air fryer. Cook the chicken drumsticks for 20 minutes at 190°C.

Sweet Chicken Wings

Prep time: 10 minutes | Cook time: 16 minutes | Serves 4

- 1-pound chicken wings
- 1 tablespoon taco seasonings
- 1 tablespoon Erythritol
- 1 tablespoon coconut oil, melted

1. Mix chicken wings with taco seasonings, Erythritol, and coconut oil.
2. Put the chicken wings in the air fryer basket or wire rack and cook them at 190°C for 16 minutes.

Lemongrass Hens

Prep time: 20 minutes | Cook time: 65 minutes | Serves 4

- 14 oz hen (chicken)
- 1 teaspoon lemongrass
- 1 teaspoon ground coriander
- 1 oz celery stalk, chopped
- 1 teaspoon dried Coriander
- 3 spring onions, diced
- 2 tablespoons avocado oil
- 2 tablespoons lime juice
- ½ teaspoon lemon zest, grated
- 1 teaspoon salt
- 1 tablespoon apple cider vinegar
- 1 teaspoon chili powder
- ½ teaspoon ground black pepper

1. In the mixing bowl mix up lemongrass, ground coriander, dried Coriander, lime juice, lemon zest, salt, apple cider vinegar, and ground black pepper. Then add spring onions and celery stalk.
2. After this, rub the hen with the spice mixture and leave for 10 minutes to marinate. Meanwhile, preheat the air fryer to 190°C.
3. Put the hen in the air fryer and cook it for 55 minutes. Then flip it on another side and cook for 10 minutes more.

Basil Chicken Wings

Prep time: 5 minutes | Cook time: 30 minutes| Serves 4

- 2 pounds of chicken wings
- 1 tablespoon dried basil
- 1 teaspoon salt
- 1 tablespoon avocado oil

1. Sprinkle the chicken wings with dried basil, salt, and avocado oil.
2. Put the chicken wings in the air fryer basket or wire rack and cook at 180°C for 30 minutes.

Smoked Paprika Chicken

Prep time: 10 minutes | Cook time: 20 minutes| Serves 4

- 2-pounds chicken breast, skinless, boneless
- 1 tablespoon smoked paprika
- 1 teaspoon coconut oil, melted
- 1 tablespoon apple cider vinegar

1. In the shallow bowl, mix coconut oil with apple cider vinegar, and smoked paprika.
2. Carefully brush the chicken breast with smoked paprika mixture.
3. Then put the chicken in the air fryer and cook it at 190°C for 20 minutes. Flip the chicken on another side after 10 minutes of cooking.

Coated Chicken

Prep time: 15 minutes | Cook time: 20 minutes| Serves 6

- 3-pounds chicken breast, skinless, boneless
- 1 tablespoon coconut shred
- 2 tablespoons scratchings
- 1 teaspoon ground black pepper
- 2 eggs, beaten
- 1 tablespoon avocado oil

1. In the shallow bowl, mix coconut shred with pork rinds, and ground black pepper.
2. Then cut the chicken breasts into 6 servings and dip in the eggs.
3. Coat the chicken in the coconut shred mixture and put it in the air fryer basket or wire rack.
4. Then sprinkle the chicken with avocado oil and cook at 190°C for 20 minutes.

Ginger Drumsticks

Prep time: 5 minutes | Cook time: 20 minutes| Serves 4

- 1 teaspoon ground ginger
- ½ teaspoon ground cinnamon
- 1 tablespoon olive oil
- ½ teaspoon onion powder
- 2-pounds chicken drumsticks

1. Mix the chicken drumsticks with onion powder, olive oil, ground cinnamon, and ground ginger.
2. Put them in the air fryer basket or wire rack and cook at 190°C for 20 minutes.

BBQ Wings
Prep time: 10 minutes | Cook time: 20 minutes| Serves 4

- 2-pound chicken wings
- 1 cup BBQ sauce
- 1 teaspoon olive oil

1. Mix BBQ sauce with olive oil.
2. Brush the chicken wings carefully with the BQ sauce mixture and put it in the air fryer.
3. Cook the chicken wings for 9 minutes per side at 190°C.

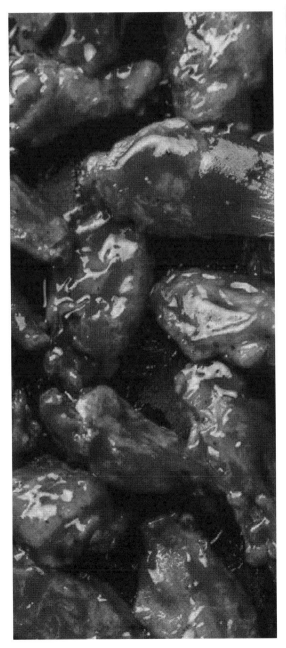

Asparagus Chicken
Prep time: 15 minutes | Cook time: 30 minutes| Serves 4

- 1 cup asparagus, chopped
- 1-pound chicken thighs, skinless, boneless
- 1 teaspoon onion powder
- 1 oz scallions, chopped
- 1 tablespoon coconut oil, melted
- 1 teaspoon smoked paprika

1. Mix chicken thighs with onion powder, coconut oil, and smoked paprika.
2. Put the chicken thighs in the air fryer and cook at 200°C for 20 minutes.
3. Then flip the chicken thighs on another side and top with chopped asparagus and scallions.
4. Cook the meal for 5 minutes more.

Nutmeg Chicken Fillets

Prep time: 15 minutes | Cook time: 12 minutes| Serves 4

- 16 oz chicken fillets
- 1 teaspoon ground nutmeg
- 1 tablespoon avocado oil
- ½ teaspoon salt

1. Mix ground nutmeg with avocado oil and salt.
2. Then rub the chicken fillet with a nutmeg mixture and put it in the air fryer basket or wire rack.
3. Cook the meal at 200°C for 12 minutes.

Sesame Chicken with Sweet Wasabi

Prep time: 5 minutes | Cook time: 16 minutes | Serves 2

- 2 tablespoon wasabi
- 1 tablespoon agave syrup
- 2 teaspoon black sesame seeds
- Salt and black pepper to taste
- 2 chicken breasts, cut into large chunks

1. In a bowl, mix wasabi, agave syrup, sesame seed, salt, and pepper. Rub the mixture onto the breasts.
2. Arrange the breasts on a greased frying basket and cook for 16 minutes, turning once halfway through.

Crunchy Coconut Chicken with Berry Sauce

Prep time: 5 minutes | Cook time: 16 minutes | Serves 4

- 2 cups coconut flakes
- 4 chicken breasts, cut into strips
- ½ cup cornflour
- Salt and black pepper to taste
- 2 eggs, beaten

1. Preheat air fryer to 180°C. Mix salt, pepper, and cornflour in a bowl. Line a frying basket with greaseproof paper.
2. Dip the chicken first in the cornflour, then into the eggs, and finally, coat with coconut flakes.
3. Arrange in the air fryer and Bake for 16 minutes, flipping once until crispy. Serve with berry sauce.

Turmeric Chicken Fillets with Sweet Chili

Prep time: 5 minutes | Cook time: 18 minutes | Serves 4

- 2 chicken breasts, halved
- Salt and black pepper to taste
- ¼ cup sweet chili sauce
- 1 teaspoon taste

1. Preheat air fryer to 200°C. In a bowl, add salt, black pepper, sweet chili sauce, and turmeric; mix well.
2. Lightly brush the chicken with the mixture and place it in the frying basket. Air Fry for 12 to 14 minutes, turning once halfway through. Serve with a side of steamed greens.

Avocado and Mango Chicken Breasts

Prep time: 10 minutes | Cook time: 14 minutes | Serves 2

- 2 chicken breasts
- 1 mango, chopped
- 1 avocado, sliced
- 1 red pepper, chopped
- 1 tablespoon balsamic vinegar
- 2 tablespoon olive oil
- 2 garlic cloves, minced
- ½ teaspoon dried oregano
- 1 teaspoon mustard powder
- Salt and black pepper to taste

1. In a bowl, mix garlic, olive oil, and balsamic vinegar. Add in the breasts, cover, and marinate for 2 hours.
2. Preheat the fryer to 180°C. Place the chicken in the frying basket and Air Fry for 12 to 14 minutes, flipping once.
3. Top with avocado, mango, and red pepper. Drizzle with balsamic vinegar and serve.

Baked Coconut and Mango Chicken Thighs

Prep time: 5 minutes | Cook time: 14 minutes | Serves 4

- 1 tablespoon curry powder
- 4 tablespoon mango chutney
- Salt and black pepper to taste
- ¾ cup coconut, shredded
- 1 pound (454 g) chicken thighs

1. Preheat air fryer to 200°C. In a bowl, mix curry powder, mango chutney, salt, and black pepper.
2. Brush the thighs with the glaze and roll the chicken thighs in desiccated coconut.
3. Grease a baking dish with cooking spray and arrange the thing in. Bake them in the air fryer for 12 to 14 minutes, turning once, until golden brown.

Sweet Mustard Chicken Thighs

Prep time: 5 minutes | Cook time: 18 minutes | Serves 4

- 4 chicken thighs, skin-on
- 1 tablespoon honey
- 1 teaspoon Dijon mustard
- Salt and garlic powder to taste

1. In a bowl, mix honey, mustard, garlic powder, and salt.
2. Brush the thighs with the mixture and Air Fry them for 16 minutes at 200°C, turning once halfway through. Serve hot.

Chapter 5
Meats

Dill-Thyme Beef Steak

Prep time: 5 minutes | Cook time: 26 minutes | Serves 6

- 1 teaspoon dried dill
- 1 teaspoon dried thyme
- 1 teaspoon garlic powder
- 2 pounds (907 g) beef steak
- 3 tablespoons butter

1. Preheat the air fryer to 200°C.
2. Combine the dill, thyme, and garlic powder in a small bowl, and massage into the steak.
3. Bake the steak in the air fryer for 24 minutes, then remove, shred, and return to the air fryer.
4. Add the butter and bake the shredded steak for a further 2 minutes at 180°C. Make sure the beef is coated in the butter before serving.

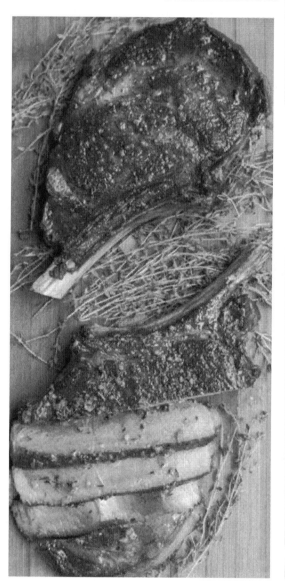

Dijon Mustard Pork Tenderloin

Prep time: 5 minutes | Cook time: 12 minutes | Serves 6

- 2 large egg whites
- 1½ tablespoons Dijon mustard
- 2 cups crushed pretzel crumbs
- 1½ pounds (680 g) pork tenderloin, cut into ¼-pound (113-g) sections
- Cooking spray

1. Preheat the air fryer to 190°C. Spritz the baking pan with cooking spray.
2. Whisk the egg whites with Dijon mustard in a bowl until bubbly. Pour the pretzel crumbs in a separate bowl.
3. Dredge the pork tenderloin in the egg white mixture and press to coat. Shake the excess off and roll the tenderloin over the pretzel crumbs.
4. Arrange the well-coated pork tenderloin in batches in a single layer in the pan and spritz with cooking spray.
5. Bake for 12 minutes or until the pork is golden brown and crispy. Flip the pork halfway through. Repeat with remaining pork sections.
6. Serve immediately.

Dijon-Lemon Pork Tenderloin

Prep time: 10 minutes | Cook time: 30 minutes | Serves 4 to 6

- ¼ cup olive oil
- ¼ cup soy sauce
- ¼ cup freshly squeezed lemon juice
- 1 garlic clove, minced
- 1 tablespoon Dijon mustard
- 1 teaspoon salt
- ½ teaspoon freshly ground black pepper
- 2 pounds (907 g) pork tenderloin

1. In a large mixing bowl, make the marinade: Mix the olive oil, soy sauce, lemon juice, minced garlic, Dijon mustard, salt, and pepper. Reserve ¼ cup of the marinade.
2. Put the tenderloin in a large bowl and pour the remaining marinade over the meat. Cover and marinate in the refrigerator for about 1 hour.
3. Preheat the air fryer to 200°C.
4. Put the marinated pork tenderloin into the baking pan. Bake for 10 minutes. Flip the pork and baste it with half of the reserved marinade. Bake for 10 minutes more.
5. Flip the pork, then baste with the remaining marinade. Bake for another 10 minutes, for a total cooking time of 30 minutes.
6. Serve immediately.

Beef and Carrot Meatballs

Prep time: 10 minutes | Cook time: 14 minutes | Serves 8

- 1 pound (454 g) minced beef
- 1 egg, beaten
- 2 carrots, shredded
- 2 bread slices, crumbled
- 1 small onion, minced
- ½ teaspoons garlic salt
- Pepper and salt, to taste
- 1 cup tomato sauce
- 2 cups pasta sauce

1. Preheat the air fryer to 200°C.
2. In a bowl, combine the minced beef, egg, carrots, crumbled bread, onion, garlic salt, pepper and salt.
3. Divide the mixture into equal amounts and shape each one into a small meatball.
4. Put them in the baking pan and bake for 8 minutes.
5. Transfer the meatballs to an air fryer-safe dish and top with the tomato sauce and pasta sauce.
6. Set the dish into the air fryer and allow to bake at 180°C for 6 more minutes. Serve hot.

Pork and Mushroom Rolls with Teriyaki

Prep time: 10 minutes | Cook time: 10 minutes | Serves 6

- 4 tablespoons Demerara sugar
- 4 tablespoons mirin
- 4 tablespoons soy sauce
- 1 teaspoon almond flour
- 2-inch ginger, chopped
- 6 (4-ounce / 113-g) pork belly slices
- 6 ounces (170 g) Enoki mushrooms

1. Mix the Demerara sugar, mirin, soy sauce, almond flour, and ginger together until Demerara sugar dissolves.
2. Take pork belly slices and wrap around a bundle of mushrooms. Brush each roll with teriyaki sauce. Chill for half an hour.
3. Preheat the air fryer to 180°C and add marinated pork rolls to the baking pan.
4. Bake for 10 minutes. Flip the rolls halfway through.
5. Serve immediately.

Pork Ribs with Honey-Soy Sauce

Prep time: 5 minutes | Cook time: 36 minutes | Serves 4

- ¼ cup soy sauce
- ¼ cup honey
- 1 teaspoon garlic powder
- 1 teaspoon ground dried ginger
- 4 (8-ounce / 227-g) boneless country-style pork ribs
- Cooking spray

1. Preheat the air fryer to 190°C. Spritz the baking pan with cooking spray.
2. Make the teriyaki sauce: Combine the soy sauce, honey, garlic powder, and ginger in a bowl. Stir to mix well.
3. Brush the ribs with half of the teriyaki sauce, then arrange the ribs in the pan. Spritz with cooking spray. You may need to work in batches to avoid overcrowding.
4. Bake for 36 minutes or until the internal temperature of the ribs reaches at least 60°C. Brush the ribs with remaining teriyaki sauce and flip halfway through.
5. Serve immediately.

Paprika Lamb Chops with Sage

Prep time: 5 minutes | Cook time: 30 minutes | Serves 4

- 1 cup plain flour
- 2 teaspoons dried sage leaves
- 2 teaspoons garlic powder
- 1 tablespoon mild paprika
- 1 tablespoon salt
- 4 (6-ounce / 170-g) bone-in lamb shoulder chops, fat trimmed
- Cooking spray

1. Preheat the air fryer to 200°C and spritz the baking pan with cooking spray.
2. Combine the flour, sage leaves, garlic powder, paprika, and salt in a large bowl. Stir to mix well. Dunk in the lamb chops and toss to coat well.
3. Arrange the lamb chops in a single layer in the pan and spritz with cooking spray. Bake for 30 minutes or until the chops are golden brown and reaches your desired doneness. Flip the chops halfway through.
4. Serve immediately.

Lemongrass Pork Chops with Fish Sauce

Prep time: 15 minutes | Cook time: 15 minutes | Serves 2

- 1 tablespoon chopped shallot
- 1 tablespoon chopped garlic
- 1 tablespoon fish sauce
- 3 tablespoons lemongrass
- 1 teaspoon soy sauce
- 1 tablespoon Demerara sugar
- 1 tablespoon olive oil
- 1 teaspoon ground black pepper
- 2 pork chops

1. Combine shallot, garlic, fish sauce, lemongrass, soy sauce, Demerara sugar, olive oil, and pepper in a bowl. Stir to mix well.
2. Put the pork chops in the bowl. Toss to coat well. Place the bowl in the refrigerator to marinate for 2 hours.
3. Preheat the air fryer to 200°C.
4. Remove the pork chops from the bowl and discard the marinade. Transfer the chops into the air fryer.
5. Bake for 15 minutes or until lightly browned. Flip the pork chops halfway through the cooking time.
6. Remove the pork chops from the air fryer and serve hot.

Lamb Kofta with Mint

Prep time: 25 minutes | Cook time: 12 minutes | Serves 4

- 1 pound (454 g) ground lamb
- 1 tablespoon ras el hanout (North African spice)
- ½ teaspoon ground coriander
- 1 teaspoon onion powder
- 1 teaspoon garlic powder
- 1 teaspoon cumin
- 2 tablespoons mint, chopped
- Salt and ground black pepper, to taste

SPECIAL EQUIPMENT:

- 4 bamboo skewers

1. Combine the ground lamb, ras el hanout, coriander, onion powder, garlic powder, cumin, mint, salt, and ground black pepper in a large bowl. Stir to mix well.
2. Transfer the mixture into banger molds and sit the bamboo skewers in the mixture. Refrigerate for 15 minutes.
3. Preheat air fryer to 200°C. Spritz the baking pan with cooking spray.
4. Place the lamb skewers in the preheated air fryer and spritz with cooking spray.
5. Bake for 12 minutes or until the lamb is well browned. Flip the lamb skewers halfway through.
6. Serve immediately.

Cheddar Prosciutto and Potato Salad

Prep time: 10 minutes | Cook time: 8 minutes | Serves 8

SALAD:

- 4 pounds (1.8 kg) potatoes, boiled and cubed
- 15 slices prosciutto, diced
- 2 cups shredded Cheddar cheese

DRESSING:

- 15 ounces (425 g) Soured cream
- 2 tablespoons mayonnaise
- 1 teaspoon salt
- 1 teaspoon black pepper
- 1 teaspoon dried basil

1. Preheat the air fryer to 190°C.
2. Put the potatoes, prosciutto, and Cheddar in a baking dish. Put it in the air fryer and bake for 8 minutes.
3. In a separate bowl, mix the Soured cream, mayonnaise, salt, pepper, and basil using a whisk.
4. Coat the salad with the dressing and serve.

Crispy Baked Venison

Prep time: 10 minutes | Cook time: 12 minutes | Serves 4

- 2 eggs
- ¼ cup milk
- 1 cup wholemeal flour
- ½ teaspoon salt
- ¼ teaspoon ground black pepper
- 1 pound (454 g) venison backstrap, sliced
- Cooking spray

1. Preheat the air fryer to 200°C and spritz the baking pan with cooking spray.
2. Whisk the eggs with milk in a large bowl. Combine the flour with salt and ground black pepper in a shallow dish.
3. Dredge the venison in the flour first, then into the egg mixture. Shake the excess off and roll the venison back over the flour to coat well.
4. Arrange half of the venison in the pan and spritz with cooking spray.
5. Bake for 12 minutes or until the internal temperature of the venison reaches at least 60°C for medium rare. Flip the venison halfway through. Repeat with remaining venison.
6. Serve immediately.

Panko Breaded Wasabi Spam

Prep time: 5 minutes | Cook time: 12 minutes | Serves 3

- ⅔ cup plain flour
- 2 large eggs
- 1½ tablespoons wasabi paste
- 2 cups panko bread crumbs
- 6½-inch-thick spam slices
- Cooking spray

1. Preheat the air fryer to 200°C and spritz the baking pan with cooking spray.
2. Pour the flour in a shallow plate. Whisk the eggs with wasabi in a large bowl. Pour the panko in a separate shallow plate.
3. Dredge the spam slices in the flour first, then dunk in the egg mixture, and then roll the spam over the panko to coat well. Shake the excess off.
4. Arrange the spam slices in a single layer in the pan and spritz with cooking spray.
5. Bake for 15 minutes or until the spam slices are golden and crispy. Flip the spam slices halfway through.
6. Serve immediately.

Orange Pork Ribs with Garlic
Prep time: 1 hour 10 minutes | Cook time: 30 minutes | Serves 6

- 2½ pounds (1.1 kg) boneless country-style pork ribs, cut into 2-inch pieces
- 3 tablespoons olive brine
- 1 tablespoon minced fresh oregano leaves
- ⅓ cup orange juice
- 1 teaspoon ground cumin
- 1 tablespoon minced garlic
- 1 teaspoon salt
- 1 teaspoon ground black pepper
- Cooking spray

1. Combine all the ingredients in a large bowl. Toss to coat the pork ribs well. Wrap the bowl in plastic and refrigerate for at least an hour to marinate.
2. Preheat the air fryer to 200°C and spritz the baking pan with cooking spray.
3. Arrange the marinated pork ribs in a single layer in the pan and spritz with cooking spray.
4. Bake for 30 minutes or until well browned. Flip the ribs halfway through.
5. Serve immediately.

Smoky Beef with Jalapeño Peppers
Prep time: 10 minutes | Cook time: 45 minutes | Serves 8

- 2 pounds (907 g) beef, at room temperature
- 2 tablespoons extra-virgin olive oil
- 1 teaspoon sea salt flakes
- 1 teaspoon ground black pepper
- 1 teaspoon smoked paprika
- Few dashes of liquid smoke
- 2 jalapeño peppers, thinly sliced

1. Preheat the air fryer to 170°C.
2. With kitchen towels, pat the beef dry.
3. Massage the extra-virgin olive oil, salt, black pepper, and paprika into the meat. Cover with liquid smoke.
4. Put the beef in the air fryer and bake for 30 minutes. Flip the beef over and allow to bake for another 15 minutes.
5. When cooked through, serve topped with sliced jalapeños.

Greek Lamb Rack

Prep time: 5 minutes | Cook time: 10 minutes | Serves 4

- ¼ cup freshly squeezed lemon juice
- 1 teaspoon oregano
- 2 teaspoons minced fresh rosemary
- 1 teaspoon minced fresh thyme
- 2 tablespoons minced garlic
- Salt and freshly ground black pepper, to taste
- 2 to 4 tablespoons olive oil
- 1 lamb rib rack (7 to 8 ribs)

1. Select the ROAST function and preheat Air Fryer to 180°C.
2. In a small mixing bowl, combine the lemon juice, oregano, rosemary, thyme, garlic, salt, pepper, and olive oil and mix well.
3. Rub the mixture over the lamb, covering all the meat. Put the rack of lamb in the air fryer oven. Roast for 10 minutes. Flip the rack halfway through.
4. After 10 minutes, measure the internal temperature of the rack of lamb reaches at least 60°C.
5. Serve immediately.

Beef Chuck Cheeseburgers

Prep time: 10 minutes | Cook time: 15 minutes | Serves 4

- ¾ pound (340 g) minced beef chuck
- 1 envelope onion soup mix
- flake salt and freshly ground black pepper, to taste
- 1 teaspoon paprika
- 4 slices Parmesan Cheese
- 4 ciabatta rolls

1. In a bowl, stir together the ground chuck, onion soup mix, salt, black pepper, and paprika to combine well.
2. Take four equal portions of the mixture and mold each one into a patty. Transfer to the air fryer oven. Select the AIR FRY function and cook at 200°C for 10 minutes.
3. Put the slices of cheese on the top of the burgers.
4. Air fry for another minute before serving on ciabatta rolls.

Cheese Crusted Chops

Prep time: 10 minutes | Cook time: 12 minutes | Serves 4 to 6

- ¼ teaspoon pepper
- ½ teaspoons salt
- 4 to 6 thick boneless pork chops
- 1 cup pork rind crumbs
- ¼ teaspoon chili powder
- ½ teaspoons onion powder
- 1 teaspoon smoked paprika
- 2 beaten eggs
- 3 tablespoons grated Parmesan cheese
- Cooking spray

1. Rub the pepper and salt on both sides of pork chops.
2. In a food processor, pulse scratchings into crumbs. Mix crumbs with chili powder, onion powder, and paprika in a bowl.
3. Beat eggs in another bowl.
4. Dip pork chops into eggs then into pork rind crumb mixture.
5. Spritz the air fryer basket or wire rack with cooking spray and add pork chops to the air fryer basket or wire rack.
6. Select the AIR FRY function and cook at 200°C for 12 minutes.
7. Serve garnished with the Parmesan cheese.

Crumbed Golden Filet Mignon

Prep time: 15 minutes | Cook time: 12 minutes | Serves 4

- ½ pound (227 g) filet mignon
- Sea salt and ground black pepper, to taste
- ½ teaspoon cayenne pepper
- 1 teaspoon dried basil
- 1 teaspoon dried rosemary
- 1 teaspoon dried thyme
- 1 tablespoon sesame oil
- 1 small egg, whisked
- ½ cup bread crumbs

1. Cover the filet mignon with the salt, black pepper, cayenne pepper, basil, rosemary, and thyme. Coat with sesame oil.
2. Put the egg in a shallow plate.
3. Pour the bread crumbs in another plate.
4. Dip the filet mignon into the egg. Roll it into the crumbs.
5. Transfer the steak to the air fryer oven. Select the AIR FRY function and cook at 180°C for 12 minutes, or until it turns golden.
6. Serve immediately.

Air Fried Beef Ribs

Prep time: 20 minutes | Cook time: 8 minutes | Serves 4

- 1 pound (454 g) meaty beef ribs, rinsed and drained
- 3 tablespoons apple cider vinegar
- 1 cup coriander, finely chopped
- 1 tablespoon fresh basil leaves, chopped
- 2 garlic cloves, finely chopped
- 1 chipotle powder
- 1 teaspoon fennel seeds
- 1 teaspoon hot paprika
- flake salt and black pepper, to taste
- ½ cup vegetable oil

1. Coat the ribs with the remaining ingredients and refrigerate for at least 3 hours.
2. Separate the ribs from the marinade and put them in the air fryer basket or wire rack.
3. Select the AIR FRY function and cook at 180°C for 8 minutes.
4. Pour the remaining marinade over the ribs before serving.

Mexican Pork Chops

Prep time: 5 minutes | Cook time: 15 minutes | Serves 2

- ¼ teaspoon dried oregano
- 1½ teaspoons taco seasoning mix
- 2 (4-ounce / 113-g) boneless pork chops
- 2 tablespoons unsalted butter, divided

1. Combine the dried oregano and taco seasoning in a small bowl and rub the mixture into the pork chops. Brush the chops with 1 tablespoon butter. Transfer to the air fryer basket or wire rack.
2. Select the AIR FRY function and cook at 200°C for 15 minutes, turning them over halfway through to air fry on the other side.
3. When the chops are a brown colour, check the internal temperature has reached 60°C and remove from the air fryer oven. Serve with a garnish of remaining butter.

Chapter 6
Fish and Seafood

Sriracha-Glazed Salmon Fillet

Prep time: 5 minutes | Cook time: 6 minutes | Serves 4

- 1 cup sriracha
- Juice of 2 lemons
- ¼ cup honey
- 4 (6-ounce / 170-g) skinless salmon fillets
- Chives, chopped, for garnish

1. Place the sriracha, lemon juice, and honey in a large resealable plastic bag or container. Add the salmon fillets and coat evenly. Refrigerate for 30 minutes.
2. Insert the Grill Grate and close the hood. Select GRILL, set the temperature to MAX, and set the time to 8 minutes. Select START/STOP to begin preheating.
3. When the unit beeps to signify it has preheated, place the fillets on the Grill Grate, gently pressing them down to maximize grill marks. Close the hood and cook for 6 minutes. (There is no need to flip the fish during cooking.)
4. After 6 minutes, check the fillets for doneness; the internal temperature should read at least 140°F (60°C) on a food thermometer. If necessary, close the hood and continue cooking up to 2 minutes more.
5. When cooking is complete, remove the fillets from the grill. Plate, and garnish with the chives.

Swordfish Steak in Caper Sauce

Prep time: 10 minutes | Cook time: 12 minutes | Serves 4

- 1 tablespoon freshly squeezed lemon juice
- 1 tablespoon extra-virgin olive oil
- Sea salt, to taste
- Freshly ground black pepper, to taste
- 4 fresh (8-ounce / 227-g) swordfish steaks, about 1-inch thick
- 4 tablespoons unsalted butter
- 1 lemon, sliced crosswise into 8 slices
- 2 tablespoons capers, drained

1. In a large shallow bowl, whisk together the lemon juice and oil. Season the swordfish steaks with salt and pepper on each side, and place them in the oil mixture. Turn to coat both sides. Refrigerate for 15 minutes.
2. Insert the Grill Grate and close the hood. Select GRILL, set the temperature to MAX, and set the time to 8 minutes. Select START/STOP to begin preheating.
3. When the unit beeps to signify it has preheated, place the swordfish on the Grill Grate. Close the hood and cook for 9 minutes. (There is no need to flip the swordfish during cooking.)
4. While the swordfish cooks, melt the butter in a small saucepan over medium heat. Stir and cook for about 3 minutes, until the butter has slightly browned. Add the lemon slices and capers to the pan, and cook for 1 minute. Turn off the heat.
5. Remove the swordfish from the grill and transfer it to a cutting board. Slice the fish into thick strips, transfer to serving platter, pour the caper sauce over the top, and serve immediately.

New England Cod Fillet Sandwich

Prep time: 15 minutes | Cook time: 15 minutes | Serves 4

- 2 large eggs
- 10 ounces (284 g) beer (an ale, IPA, or any type you have on hand will work)
- 1½ teaspoons chili sauce
- 1½ cups cornflour
- 1½ cups plain flour
- 1 teaspoon sea salt
- 1 teaspoon freshly ground black pepper
- 4 fresh (5- or 6-ounce / 142- or 170-g) cod fillets
- Nonstick cooking spray
- 4 soft rolls, sliced
- Tartar sauce
- Lettuce leaves
- Lemon wedges

1. Insert the Crisper Basket and close the hood. Select AIR CRISP, set the temperature to 190°C, and set the time to 15 minutes. Select START/STOP to begin preheating.
2. While the unit is preheating, whisk together the eggs, beer, and chili sauce in a large shallow bowl. In a separate large bowl, whisk together the cornflour, flour, salt, and pepper.
3. One at a time, coat the cod fillets in the egg mixture, then dredge them in the flour mixture and coat on all sides. Repeat with the remaining cod fillets.
4. When the unit beeps to signify it has preheated, spray the Crisper Basket with the cooking spray. Place the fish fillets in the air fryer basket or wire rack and coat them with the cooking spray. Close the hood and cook for 15 minutes.
5. After 15 minutes, check the fish for desired crispiness. Remove from the air fryer basket or wire rack.
6. Assemble the sandwiches by spreading tartar sauce on one half of each of the sliced rolls. Add one fish fillet and lettuce leaves, and serve with lemon wedges.

Crab Cake with Cajun Aioli

Prep time: minutes | Cook time: 10 minutes | Serves 4

- 1 egg
- ½ cup mayonnaise, plus 3 tablespoons
- Juice of ½ lemon
- 1 tablespoon minced scallions (green parts only)
- 1 teaspoon Old Bay seasoning
- 8 ounces (227 g) lump crabmeat
- ⅓ cup bread crumbs
- Nonstick cooking spray
- ½ teaspoon cayenne pepper
- ¼ teaspoon paprika
- ¼ teaspoon garlic powder
- ¼ teaspoon chili powder
- ¼ teaspoon onion powder
- ¼ teaspoon freshly ground black pepper
- ⅛ teaspoon ground nutmeg

1. Insert the Crisper Basket and close the hood. Select AIR CRISP, set the temperature to 190°C, and set the time to 10 minutes. Select START/STOP to begin preheating.
2. While the unit is preheating, in a medium bowl, whisk together the egg, 3 tablespoons of mayonnaise, lemon juice, scallions, and Old Bay seasoning. Gently stir in the crabmeat, making sure not to break up the meat into small pieces. Add the bread crumbs, and gradually mix them in. Form the mixture into four patties.
3. When the unit beeps to signify it has preheated, place the crab cakes in the air fryer basket or wire rack and coat them with the cooking spray. Close the hood and cook for 10 minutes.
4. While the crab cakes are cooking, in a small bowl, mix the remaining ½ cup of mayonnaise, cayenne pepper, paprika, garlic powder, chili powder, onion powder, black pepper, and nutmeg until fully combined.
5. When cooking is complete, serve the crab cakes with the Cajun aioli spooned on top.

Homemade Fish fingers

Prep time: 10 minutes | Cook time: 8 minutes | Makes 8 Fish fingers

- 8 ounces (227 g) fish fillets (pollock or cod), cut into ½×3-inch strips
- Salt, to taste (optional)
- ½ cup plain bread crumbs
- Cooking spray

1. Season the fish strips with salt to taste, if desired.
2. Place the bread crumbs on a plate. Roll the fish strips in the bread crumbs to coat. Spritz the fish strips with cooking spray.
3. Arrange the fish strips in the air fry basket in a single layer.
4. Select Air Fry, set temperature to 200°C, and set time to 8 minutes. Select Start/Stop to begin preheating.
5. Once preheated, place the air fryer basket or wire rack on the air fry position.
6. When cooking is complete, they should be golden brown. Remove from the oven and cool for 5 minutes before serving.

Parmesan-Crusted Hake with Garlic Sauce

Prep time: 5 minutes | Cook time: 10 minutes | Serves 3

FISH:

- 6 tablespoons mayonnaise
- 1 tablespoon fresh lime juice
- 1 teaspoon Dijon mustard
- 1 cup grated Parmesan cheese
- Salt, to taste
- ¼ teaspoon ground black pepper, or more to taste
- 3 hake fillets, patted dry
- Nonstick cooking spray
- Garlic Sauce:
- ¼ cup plain Greek yogurt
- 2 tablespoons olive oil
- 2 cloves garlic, minced
- ½ teaspoon minced tarragon leaves

1. Mix the mayo, lime juice, and mustard in a shallow bowl and whisk to combine. In another shallow bowl, stir together the grated Parmesan cheese, salt, and pepper.
2. Dredge each fillet in the mayo mixture, then roll them in the cheese mixture until they are evenly coated on both sides.
3. Spray the air fry basket with nonstick cooking spray. Place the fillets in the air fryer basket or wire rack.
4. Select Air Fry, set temperature to 200°C, and set time to 10 minutes. Select Start/Stop to begin preheating.
5. Once preheated, place the air fryer basket or wire rack on the air fry position. Flip the fillets halfway through the cooking time.
6. Meanwhile, in a small bowl, whisk all the ingredients for the sauce until well incorporated.
7. When cooking is complete, the fish should flake apart with a fork. Remove the fillets from the oven and serve warm alongside the sauce.

Chili Prawns

Prep time: 10 minutes | Cook time: 8 minutes | Serves 2

- 8 prawns, cleaned
- Salt and black pepper, to taste
- ½ teaspoon ground cayenne pepper
- ½ teaspoon garlic powder
- ½ teaspoon ground cumin
- ½ teaspoon red chili flakes
- Cooking spray

1. Spritz the air fry basket with cooking spray.
2. Toss the remaining ingredients in a large bowl until the prawns are well coated.
3. Spread the coated prawns evenly in the air fry basket and spray them with cooking spray.
4. Select Air Fry, set temperature to 170°C, and set time to 8 minutes. Select Start/Stop to begin preheating.
5. Once preheated, place the air fryer basket or wire rack on the air fry position. Flip the prawns halfway through the cooking time.
6. When cooking is complete, the prawns should be pink. Remove the prawns from the oven to a plate.

Parmesan Fish Fillets

Prep time: 8 minutes | Cook time: 17 minutes | Serves 4

- ⅓ cup grated Parmesan cheese
- ½ teaspoon fennel seed
- ½ teaspoon tarragon
- ⅓ teaspoon mixed peppercorns
- 2 eggs, beaten
- 4 (4-ounce / 113-g) fish fillets, halved
- 2 tablespoons dry white wine
- 1 teaspoon seasoned salt

1. Place the grated Parmesan cheese, fennel seed, tarragon, and mixed peppercorns in a food processor and pulse for about 20 seconds until well combined. Transfer the cheese mixture to a shallow dish.
2. Place the beaten eggs in another shallow dish.
3. Drizzle the dry white wine over the top of fish fillets. Dredge each fillet in the beaten eggs on both sides, shaking off any excess, then roll them in the cheese mixture until fully coated. Season with the salt.
4. Arrange the fillets in the air fry basket.
5. Select Air Fry, set temperature to 345°F (174°C), and set time to 17 minutes. Select Start/Stop to begin preheating.
6. Once preheated, place the air fryer basket or wire rack on the air fry position. Flip the fillets once halfway through the cooking time.
7. When cooking is complete, the fish should be cooked through no longer translucent. Remove from the oven and cool for 5 minutes before serving.

Cajun Catfish Cakes with Cheese

Prep time: 5 minutes | Cook time: 15 minutes | Serves 4

- 2 catfish fillets
- 3 ounces (85 g) butter
- 1 cup shredded Parmesan cheese
- 1 cup shredded Emmethaler
- ½ cup buttermilk
- 1 teaspoon baking powder
- 1 teaspoon baking soda
- 1 teaspoon Cajun seasoning

1. Bring a pot of salted water to a boil. Add the catfish fillets to the boiling water and let them boil for 5 minutes until they become opaque.
2. Remove the fillets from the pot to a mixing bowl and flake them into small pieces with a fork.
3. Add the remaining ingredients to the bowl of fish and stir until well incorporated.
4. Divide the fish mixture into 12 equal portions and shape each portion into a patty. Place the patties in the air fry basket.
5. Select Air Fry, set temperature to 190°C, and set time to 15 minutes. Select Start/Stop to begin preheating.
6. Once preheated, place the air fryer basket or wire rack on the air fry position. Flip the patties halfway through the cooking time.
7. When cooking is complete, the patties should be golden brown and cooked through. Remove from the oven. Let the patties sit for 5 minutes and serve.

Coconut Chili Fish Curry

Prep time: 10 minutes | Cook time: 22 minutes | Serves 4

- 2 tablespoons sunflower oil, divided
- 1 pound (454 g) fish, chopped
- 1 ripe tomato, pureéd
- 2 red chilies, chopped
- 1 shallot, minced
- 1 garlic clove, minced
- 1 cup coconut milk
- 1 tablespoon coriander powder
- 1 teaspoon red curry paste
- ½ teaspoon fenugreek seeds
- Salt and white pepper, to taste

1. Coat the air fry basket with 1 tablespoon of sunflower oil. Place the fish in the air fry basket.
2. Select Air Fry, set temperature to 190°C, and set time to 10 minutes. Select Start/Stop to begin preheating.
3. Once preheated, place the air fryer basket or wire rack on the air fry position. Flip the fish halfway through the cooking time.
4. When cooking is complete, transfer the cooked fish to a baking pan greased with the remaining 1 tablespoon of sunflower oil. Stir in the remaining ingredients.
5. Select Air Fry, set temperature to 180°C, and set time to 12 minutes. Select Start/Stop to begin preheating.
6. Once preheated, place the pan on the air fry position.
7. When cooking is complete, they should be heated through. Cool for 5 to 8 minutes before serving.

Browned Prawn Patties

Prep time: 15 minutes | Cook time: 12 minutes | Serves 4

- ½ pound (227 g) raw Prawn, shelled, deveined, and chopped finely
- 2 cups cooked sushi rice
- ¼ cup chopped red bell pepper
- ¼ cup chopped celery
- ¼ cup chopped green onion
- 2 teaspoons Worcestershire sauce
- ½ teaspoon salt
- ½ teaspoon garlic powder
- ½ teaspoon Old Bay seasoning
- ½ cup plain bread crumbs
- Cooking spray

1. Put all the ingredients except the bread crumbs and oil in a large bowl and stir to incorporate.
2. Scoop out the Prawn mixture and shape into 8 equal-sized patties with your hands, no more than ½-inch thick. Roll the patties in the bread crumbs on a plate and spray both sides with cooking spray. Place the patties in the air fry basket.
3. Select Air Fry, set temperature to 200°C, and set time to 12 minutes. Select Start/Stop to begin preheating.
4. Once preheated, place the air fryer basket or wire rack on the air fry position. Flip the patties halfway through the cooking time.
5. When cooking is complete, the outside should be crispy brown. Remove the air fryer basket or wire rack from the oven. Divide the patties among four plates and serve warm.

Crab Cakes with Bell Peppers

Prep time: 5 minutes | Cook time: 10 minutes | Serves 4

- 8 ounces (227 g) jumbo lump crab meat
- 1 egg, beaten
- Juice of ½ lemon
- ⅓ cup bread crumbs
- ¼ cup diced green bell pepper
- ¼ cup diced red bell pepper
- ¼ cup mayonnaise
- 1 tablespoon Old Bay seasoning
- 1 teaspoon flour
- Cooking spray

1. Make the crab cakes: Place all the ingredients except the flour and oil in a large bowl and stir until well incorporated.
2. Divide the crab mixture into four equal portions and shape each portion into a patty with your hands. Top each patty with a sprinkle of ¼ teaspoon of flour.
3. Arrange the crab cakes in the air fry basket and spritz them with cooking spray.
4. Select Air Fry, set temperature to 190°C, and set time to 10 minutes. Select Start/Stop to begin preheating.
5. Once preheated, place the air fryer basket or wire rack on the air fry position. Flip the crab cakes halfway through.
6. When cooking is complete, the cakes should be cooked through. Remove the air fryer basket or wire rack from the oven. Divide the crab cakes among four plates and serve.

Air-Fried Scallops

Prep time: 10 minutes | Cook time: 12 minutes | Serves 2

- ⅓ cup shallots, chopped
- 1½ tablespoons olive oil
- 1½ tablespoons coconut aminos
- 1 tablespoon Mediterranean seasoning mix
- ½ tablespoon balsamic vinegar
- ½ teaspoon ginger, grated
- 1 clove garlic, chopped
- 1 pound (454 g) scallops, cleaned Cooking spray
- Belgian chicory, for garnish

1. Place all the ingredients except the scallops and Belgian chicory in a small frying pan over medium heat and stir to combine. Let this mixture simmer for about 2 minutes.
2. Remove the mixture from the frying pan to a large bowl and set aside to cool.
3. Add the scallops, coating them all over, then transfer to the refrigerator to marinate for at least 2 hours.
4. When ready, place the scallops in the air fry basket in a single layer and spray with cooking spray.
5. Select Air Fry, set temperature to 345°F (174°C), and set time to 10 minutes. Select Start/Stop to begin preheating.
6. Once preheated, place the air fryer basket or wire rack on the air fry position. Flip the scallops halfway through the cooking time.
7. When cooking is complete, the scallops should be tender and opaque. Remove from the oven and serve garnished with the Belgian chicory.

Bacon-Wrapped Scallops

Prep time: 5 minutes | Cook time: 10 minutes | Serves 4

- 8 slices bacon, cut in half
- 16 sea scallops, patted dry
- Cooking spray
- Salt and freshly ground black pepper, to taste
- 16 Cocktail Sticks, soaked in water for at least 30 minutes

1. On a clean work surface, wrap half of a slice of bacon around each scallop and secure with a toothpick.
2. Lay the bacon-wrapped scallops in the air fry basket in a single layer.
3. Spritz the scallops with cooking spray and sprinkle the salt and pepper to season.
4. Select Air Fry, set temperature to 190°C, and set time to 10 minutes. Select Start/Stop to begin preheating.
5. Once preheated, place the air fryer basket or wire rack on the air fry position. Flip the scallops halfway through the cooking time.
6. When cooking is complete, the bacon should be cooked through and the scallops should be firm. Remove the scallops from the oven to a plate Serve warm.

Breaded Scallops

Prep time: 5 minutes | Cook time: 7 minutes | Serves 4

- 1 egg
- 3 tablespoons flour
- 1 cup bread crumbs
- 1 pound (454 g) fresh scallops
- 2 tablespoons olive oil
- Salt and black pepper, to taste

1. In a bowl, lightly beat the egg. Place the flour and bread crumbs into separate shallow dishes.
2. Dredge the scallops in the flour and shake off any excess. Dip the flour-coated scallops in the beaten egg and roll in the bread crumbs.
3. Brush the scallops generously with olive oil and season with salt and pepper, to taste. Transfer the scallops to the air fry basket.
4. Select Air Fry, set temperature to 180°C , and set time to 7 minutes. Select Start/Stop to begin preheating.
5. Once preheated, place the air fryer basket or wire rack on the air fry position. Flip the scallops halfway through the cooking time.
6. When cooking is complete, the scallops should reach an internal temperature of just 60°C on a meat thermometer. Remove the air fryer basket or wire rack from the oven. Let the scallops cool for 5 minutes and serve.

Easy Scallops

Prep time: 5 minutes | Cook time: 4 minutes | Serves 2

- 12 medium sea scallops, rinsed and patted dry
- 1 teaspoon fine sea salt
- ¾ teaspoon ground black pepper, plus more for garnish
- Fresh thyme leaves, for garnish (optional)
- Avocado oil spray

1. Coat the air fry basket with avocado oil spray.
2. Place the scallops in a medium bowl and spritz with avocado oil spray. Sprinkle the salt and pepper to season.
3. Transfer the seasoned scallops to the air fry basket, spacing them apart.
4. Select Air Fry, set temperature to 200°C, and set time to 4 minutes. Select Start/Stop to begin preheating.
5. Once preheated, place the air fryer basket or wire rack on the air fry position. Flip the scallops halfway through the cooking time.
6. When cooking is complete, the scallops should reach an internal temperature of just 60°C on a meat thermometer. Remove the air fryer basket or wire rack from the oven. Sprinkle the pepper and thyme leaves on top for garnish, if desired. Serve immediately.

Breaded Calamari with Lemon

Prep time: 5 minutes | Cook time: 12 minutes | Serves 4

- 2 large eggs
- 2 garlic cloves, minced
- ½ cup cornflour
- 1 cup bread crumbs
- 1 pound (454 g) calamari rings
- Cooking spray
- 1 lemon, sliced

1. In a small bowl, whisk the eggs with minced garlic. Place the cornflour and bread crumbs into separate shallow dishes.
2. Dredge the calamari rings in the cornflour, then dip in the egg mixture, shaking off any excess, finally roll them in the bread crumbs to coat well. Let the calamari rings sit for 10 minutes in the refrigerator.
3. Spritz the air fry basket with cooking spray. Transfer the calamari rings to the air fryer basket or wire rack.
4. Select Air Fry, set temperature to 200°C, and set time to 12 minutes. Select Start/Stop to begin preheating.
5. Once preheated, place the air fryer basket or wire rack on the air fry position. Stir the calamari rings once halfway through the cooking time.
6. When cooking is complete, remove the air fryer basket or wire rack from the oven. Serve the calamari rings with the lemon slices sprinkled on top.

Herbed Scallops with Vegetables

Prep time: 15 minutes | Cook time: 9 minutes | Serves 4

- 1 cup frozen peas
- 1 cup Runner Beans
- 1 cup frozen chopped broccoli
- 2 teaspoons olive oil
- ½ teaspoon dried oregano
- ½ teaspoon dried basil
- 12 ounces (340 g) sea scallops, rinsed and patted dry

1. Put the peas, Runner Beans, and broccoli in a large bowl. Drizzle with the olive oil and toss to coat well. Transfer the vegetables to the air fry basket.
2. Select Air Fry, set temperature to 200°C, and set time to 5 minutes. Select Start/Stop to begin preheating.
3. Once preheated, place the air fryer basket or wire rack on the air fry position.
4. When cooking is complete, the vegetables should be fork-tender. Transfer the vegetables to a serving bowl. Scatter with the oregano and basil and set aside.
5. Place the scallops in the air fry basket.
6. Select Air Fry, set temperature to 200°C, and set time to 4 minutes. Select Start/Stop to begin preheating.
7. Once preheated, place the air fryer basket or wire rack on the air fry position.
8. When cooking is complete, the scallops should be firm and just opaque in the center. Remove from the oven to the bowl of vegetables and toss well. Serve warm.

Garlic Prawn with Parsley

Prep time: 10 minutes | Cook time: 5 minutes | Serves 4

- 18 Prawn, shelled and deveined
- 2 garlic cloves, peeled and minced
- 2 tablespoons extra-virgin olive oil
- 2 tablespoons freshly squeezed lemon juice
- ½ cup fresh parsley, coarsely chopped
- 1 teaspoon onion powder
- 1 teaspoon lemon-pepper seasoning
- ½ teaspoon hot paprika
- ½ teaspoon salt
- ¼ teaspoon cumin powder

1. Toss all the ingredients in a mixing bowl until the Prawn are well coated.
2. Cover and allow to marinate in the refrigerator for 30 minutes.
3. When ready, transfer the Prawn to the air fry basket.
4. Select Air Fry, set temperature to 200°C, and set time to 5 minutes. Select Start/Stop to begin preheating.
5. Once preheated, place the air fryer basket or wire rack on the air fry position.
6. When cooking is complete, the Prawn should be pink on the outside and opaque in the center. Remove from the oven and serve warm.

Lemony Prawn

Prep time: 10 minutes | Cook time: 8 minutes | Serves 4

- 1 pound (454 g) Prawn, deveined
- 4 tablespoons olive oil
- 1½ tablespoons lemon juice
- 1½ tablespoons fresh parsley, roughly chopped
- 2 cloves garlic, finely minced
- 1 teaspoon crushed red pepper flakes, or more to taste
- Garlic pepper, to taste
- Sea salt flakes, to taste

1. Toss all the ingredients in a large bowl until the Prawn are coated on all sides.
2. Arrange the Prawn in the air fry basket.
3. Select Air Fry, set temperature to 200°C, and set time to 8 minutes. Select Start/Stop to begin preheating.
4. Once preheated, place the air fryer basket or wire rack on the air fry position.
5. When cooking is complete, the Prawn should be pink and cooked through. Remove from the oven and serve warm.

Chapter 7
Side Dishes

Turmeric Cauliflower Rice

Prep time: 5 minutes | Cook time: 20 minutes | Serves 4

- 1 big cauliflower, florets separated and riced
- 1 and ½ cups chicken stock
- 1 tablespoon olive oil
- Salt and black pepper to the taste
- ½ teaspoon turmeric powder

1. In a pan that fits the air fryer, combine the cauliflower with the oil and the rest of the ingredients, toss, introduce in the air fryer and cook at 180°C for 20 minutes.
2. Divide between plates and serve as a side dish.

Mushroom Cakes

Prep time: 10 minutes | Cook time: 8 minutes | Serves 4

- 9 oz mushrooms, finely chopped
- ¼ cup coconut flour
- 1 teaspoon salt
- 1 egg, beaten
- 3 oz Cheddar cheese, shredded
- 1 teaspoon dried parsley
- ½ teaspoon ground black pepper
- 1 teaspoon sesame oil
- 1 oz spring onion, chopped

1. In the mixing bowl mix up chopped mushrooms, coconut flour, salt, egg, dried parsley, ground black pepper, and minced onion. Stir the mixture until smooth and add Cheddar cheese.
2. Stir it with the help of the fork, Preheat the air fryer to 190°C. Line the air fryer pan with baking paper. With the help of the spoon make the medium size patties and put them in the pan.
3. Sprinkle the patties with sesame oil and cook for 4 minutes from each side.

Cauliflower and Tomato Bake

Prep time: 5 minutes | Cook time: 20 minutes | Serves 2

- 1 cup heavy whipping cream
- 2 tablespoons basil pesto
- Salt and black pepper to the taste
- Juice of ½ lemon
- 1 pound cauliflower, florets separated
- 4 ounces cherry tomatoes, halved
- 3 tablespoons ghee, melted
- 7 ounces cheddar cheese, grated

1. Grease a baking pan that fits the air fryer with the ghee. Add the cauliflower, lemon juice, salt, pepper, the pesto and the cream and toss gently.
2. Add the tomatoes, sprinkle the cheese on top, introduce the pan in the fryer and cook at 190°C for 20 minutes. Divide between plates and serve as a side dish.

Turmeric Tofu

Prep time: 10 minutes | Cook time: 9 minutes | Serves 2

- 6 oz tofu, cubed
- 1 teaspoon avocado oil
- 1 teaspoon apple cider vinegar
- 1 garlic clove, diced
- ¼ teaspoon ground turmeric
- ¼ teaspoon ground paprika
- ½ teaspoon dried Coriander
- ¼ teaspoon lemon zest, grated

1. In the bowl mix up avocado oil, apple cider vinegar, diced garlic, ground turmeric, paprika, Coriander, and lime zest.
2. Coat the tofu cubes in the oil mixture. Preheat the air fryer to 200°C. Put the tofu cubes in the air fryer and cook them for 9 minutes.
3. Shake the tofu cubes from time to time during cooking.

Perfect Zoodles

Prep time: 5 minutes | Cook time: 10 minutes| Serves 2

- 1 (12-inch) courgette
- special equipment:
- Spiral slicer

1. Spray the air fryer basket or wire rack with avocado oil. Preheat the air fryer to 200°C.
2. Cut the ends off the courgette to create nice even edges. If you desire completely white noodles, peel the courgette. Using a spiral slicer, cut the courgette into long, thin noodles.
3. Spread out the courgette noodles in the air fryer basket or wire rack in a single layer and cook for 8 minutes, or until soft. Remove from the air fryer and serve immediately.
4. Store leftovers in an airtight container for 4 days. Reheat in a single layer in the air fryer for 3 minutes, or until heated through.

Marinated Turmeric Cauliflower Steaks

Prep time: 5 minutes | Cook time: 20 minutes| Serves 4

- ¼ cup avocado oil
- ¼ cup lemon juice
- 2 cloves garlic, minced
- 1 teaspoon grated fresh ginger
- 1 tablespoon turmeric powder
- 1 teaspoon fine sea salt
- 1 medium head cauliflower
- Full-fat Soured cream (or Kite Hill brand almond milk yogurt for dairy-free), for serving (optional)
- Extra-virgin olive oil, for serving (optional)
- Chopped fresh Coriander leaves, for garnish (optional)

1. Preheat the air fryer to 200°C.
2. In a large shallow dish, combine the avocado oil, lemon juice, garlic, ginger, turmeric, and salt. Slice the cauliflower into ½-inch steaks and place them in the marinade. Cover and refrigerate for 20 minutes or overnight.
3. Remove the cauliflower steaks from the marinade and place them in the air fryer basket or wire rack. Cook for 15 minutes, or until tender and slightly charred on the edges.
4. Serve with Soured cream and a drizzle of olive oil, and sprinkle with chopped Coriander leaves if desired.
5. Store leftovers in an airtight container in the fridge for up to 4 days or in the freezer for up to a month. Reheat in a preheated 200°C air fryer for 5 minutes, or until warm.

Caramelized Ranch Cauliflower

Prep time: 5 minutes | Cook time: 12 minutes| Serves 4

- 4 cups cauliflower florets
- 2 tablespoons dried parsley
- 1 tablespoon plus 1 teaspoon onion powder
- 2 teaspoons garlic powder
- 1½ teaspoons dried dill weed
- 1 teaspoon dried chives
- 1 teaspoon fine sea salt or smoked salt
- 1 teaspoon ground black pepper
- Ranch Dressing, for serving (optional)

1. Preheat the air fryer to 200°C.
2. Place the cauliflower in a large bowl and spray it with avocado oil.
3. Place the parsley, onion powder, garlic powder, dill weed, chives, salt, and pepper in a small bowl and stir to combine well. Sprinkle the ranch seasoning over the cauliflower.
4. Place the cauliflower in the air fryer and cook for 12 minutes, or until tender and crisp on the edges. Serve with ranch dressing for dipping, if desired.
5. Store leftovers in an airtight container in the fridge for up to 4 days or in the freezer for up to a month. Reheat in a preheated 200°C air fryer for 5 minutes, or until crisp.

Fried Cauliflower Rice

Prep time: 5 minutes | Cook time: 10 minutes| Serves 4

- 2 cups cauliflower florets
- ⅓ cup sliced green onions, plus more for garnish
- 3 tablespoons wheat-free tamari or coconut aminos
- 1 clove garlic, smashed to a paste or minced
- 1 teaspoon grated fresh ginger
- 1 teaspoon fish sauce or fine sea salt (see Note)
- 1 teaspoon lime juice
- ⅛ teaspoon ground black pepper

1. Preheat the air fryer to 190°C.
2. Place the cauliflower in a food processor and pulse until it resembles grains of rice.
3. Place all the ingredients, including the riced cauliflower, in a large bowl and stir well to combine.
4. Transfer the cauliflower mixture to a 6-inch pie pan or a casserole dish that will fit in your air fryer. Cook for 8 minutes, or until soft, shaking halfway through. Garnish with sliced green onions before serving.
5. Store leftovers in an airtight container in the fridge for up to 4 days. Reheat in a preheated 190°C air fryer for 4 minutes, or until heated through.

Garlic Thyme Mushrooms

Prep time: 5 minutes | Cook time: 10 minutes | Serves 4

- 3 tablespoons unsalted butter (or butter-flavoured coconut oil for dairy-free), melted
- 1 (8-ounce) package button mushrooms, sliced
- 2 cloves garlic, minced
- 3 sprigs fresh thyme leaves, plus more for garnish
- ½ teaspoon fine sea salt

1. Spray the air fryer basket or wire rack with avocado oil. Preheat the air fryer to 200°C.
2. Place all the ingredients in a medium-sized bowl. Use a spoon or your hands to coat the mushroom slices.
3. Place the mushrooms in the air fryer basket or wire rack in one layer; work in batches if necessary. Cook for 10 minutes, or until slightly crispy and brown. Garnish with thyme sprigs before serving.
4. Store leftovers in an airtight container in the fridge for up to 5 days or in the freezer for up to a month. Reheat in a preheated 160°C air fryer for 5 minutes, or until heated through.

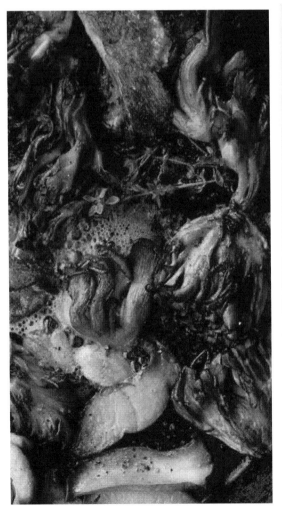

Sweet Fauxtato Casserole

Prep time: 15 minutes | Cook time: 55 minutes | Serves 6

- 2 cups cauliflower florets
- 1 cup chicken broth or water
- 1 cup tinned pumpkin puree
- ⅓ cup unsalted butter, melted (or coconut oil for dairy-free), plus more for the pan
- ¼ cup Swerve confectioners'-style sweetener or equivalent amount of liquid or powdered sweetener
- ¼ cup unsweetened, unflavoured almond milk or double cream
- 2 large eggs, beaten
- 1 teaspoon fine sea salt
- 1 teaspoon vanilla extract
- TOPPING:
- 1 cup chopped pecans
- ½ cup blanched almond flour or pecan meal
- ½ cup Swerve confectioners'-style sweetener or equivalent amount of powdered sweetener
- ⅓ cup unsalted butter, melted (or coconut oil for dairy-free)
- Chopped fresh parsley leaves, for garnish (optional)

1. Preheat the air fryer to 160°C.
2. Place the cauliflower florets in a 6-inch pie pan or a casserole dish that will fit in your air fryer. Add the broth to the pie pan. Cook in the air fryer for 20 minutes, or until the cauliflower is very tender.
3. Drain the cauliflower and transfer it to a food processor. Set the pie pan aside; you'll use it in the next step. Blend the cauliflower until very smooth. Add the pumpkin, butter, sweetener, almond milk, eggs, salt, and vanilla and puree until smooth.
4. Grease the pie pan that you cooked the cauliflower in with butter. Pour the cauliflower-pumpkin mixture into the pan. Set aside.
5. Make the topping: In a large bowl, mix together all the ingredients for the topping until well combined. Crumble the topping over the cauliflower-pumpkin mixture.
6. Cook in the air fryer for 30 to 35 minutes, until cooked through and golden brown on top. Garnish with fresh parsley before serving, if desired.
7. Store leftovers in an airtight container in the fridge for up to 4 days or in the freezer for up to a month. Reheat in a preheated 160°C air fryer for 6 minutes, or until heated through.

Spinach Artichoke Tart

Prep time: 15 minutes | Cook time: 40 minutes | Serves 6

CRUST:
- 1 cup blanched almond flour
- 1 cup grated Parmesan cheese (about 3 ounces)
- 1 large egg
- FILLING:
- 4 ounces cream cheese (½ cup), softened
- 1 (8-ounce) package frozen chopped spinach, thawed and drained
- ½ cup artichoke hearts, drained and chopped
- ⅓ cup shredded Parmesan cheese, plus more for topping
- 1 large egg
- 1 clove garlic, minced
- ¼ teaspoon fine sea salt

1. Preheat the air fryer to 160°C.
2. Make the crust: Place the almond flour and cheese in a large bowl and mix until well combined. Add the egg and mix until the dough is well combined and stiff.
3. Press the dough into a 6-inch pie pan. Bake for 8 to 10 minutes, until it starts to brown lightly.
4. Meanwhile, make the filling: Place the cream cheese in a large bowl and stir to break it up. Add the spinach, artichoke hearts, cheese, egg, garlic, and salt. Stir well to combine.
5. Pour the spinach mixture into the prebaked crust and sprinkle with additional Parmesan. Place in the air fryer and cook for 25 to 30 minutes, until cooked through.
6. Store leftovers in an airtight container in the fridge for up to 4 days or in the freezer for up to a month. Reheat in a preheated 160°C air fryer for 5 minutes, or until heated through.

Crunchy-Top Personal Mac 'n' Cheese

Prep time: 15 minutes | Cook time: 15 minutes | Serves 4

- 2 cups frozen chopped cauliflower, thawed
- 2 ounces cream cheese (¼ cup), softened
- ¼ cup shredded Gruyère or Emmethaler
- ¼ cup shredded sharp cheddar cheese
- 2 tablespoons finely diced onions
- 3 tablespoons beef broth
- ¼ teaspoon fine sea salt

TOPPING:
- ¼ cup pork dust
- ¼ cup unsalted butter, melted, plus more for greasing ramekins
- 4 slices bacon, finely diced

FOR GARNISH (OPTIONAL):
- Chopped fresh thyme or chives

1. Preheat the air fryer to 190°C.
2. Place the cauliflower on a paper towel and pat dry. Cut any large pieces of cauliflower into ½-inch pieces.
3. In a medium-sized bowl, stir together the cream cheese, Gruyère, cheddar, and onions. Slowly stir in the broth and combine well. Add the salt and stir to combine. Add the cauliflower and stir gently to mix the cauliflower into the cheese sauce.
4. Grease four 4-ounce ramekins with butter. Divide the cauliflower mixture among the ramekins, filling each three-quarters full.
5. Make the topping: In a small bowl, stir together the pork dust, butter, and bacon until well combined. Divide the topping among the ramekins.
6. Place the ramekins in the air fryer (if you're using a smaller air fryer, work in batches if necessary) and cook for 15 minutes, or until the topping is browned and the bacon is crispy.
7. Garnish with fresh thyme or chives, if desired.
8. Store leftovers in the ramekins covered with foil. Reheat in a preheated 190°C air fryer for 6 minutes, or until the cauliflower is heated through and the top is crispy.

Parmesan Flan

Prep time: 15 minutes | Cook time: 25 minutes| Serves 4

- ½ cup grated Parmesan cheese (about 1½ ounces)
- 1 cup double cream, very warm
- ⅛ teaspoon fine sea salt
- ⅛ teaspoon ground white pepper
- 1 large egg
- 1 large egg yolk
- FOR SERVING/GARNISH (OPTIONAL):
- 2 cups rocket
- 1 cup heirloom cherry tomatoes, halved
- 4 slices Italian cured beef (omit for vegetarian)
- Ground black pepper

1. Preheat the air fryer to 160°C. Grease four 4-ounce ramekins well.
2. Place the Parmesan in a medium-sized bowl and pour in the warm cream. Stir well to combine and add the salt and pepper.
3. In a separate medium-sized bowl, beat the egg and yolk until well combined. Gradually stir in the warm Parmesan mixture.
4. Pour the egg-and-cheese mixture into the prepared ramekins, cover the ramekins with foil, and place them in a casserole dish that will fit in your air fryer.
5. Pour boiling water into the casserole dish until the water reaches halfway up the sides of the ramekins. Place the casserole dish in the air fryer and bake until the flan is just set (the mixture will jiggle slightly when moved), about 25 minutes. Check after 20 minutes.
6. Let the flan rest for 15 minutes. Serve with rocket, halved cherry tomatoes, and slices of Italian cured beef, if desired. Garnish with ground black pepper, if desired.
7. Store leftovers in an airtight container in the fridge for up to 5 days. Reheat the flan in a ramekin in a preheated 160°C air fryer for 5 minutes, or until heated through.

Garlic Butter Breadsticks

Prep time: 15 minutes | Cook time: 12 minutes| Serves 1

DOUGH:
- 1¾ cups shredded mozzarella cheese (about 7 ounces)
- 2 tablespoons unsalted butter
- 1 large egg, beaten
- ¾ cup blanched almond flour
- ⅛ teaspoon fine sea salt

GARLIC BUTTER:
- 3 tablespoons unsalted butter, softened
- 2 cloves garlic, minced

TOPPING:
- ½ cup shredded Parmesan cheese (about 2 ounces)
- 1 teaspoon dried basil leaves
- 1 teaspoon dried oregano leaves
- FOR SERVING (OPTIONAL):
- ½ cup marinara sauce

1. Preheat the air fryer to 200°C. Place a piece of greaseproof paper in a 6-inch square casserole dish and spray it with avocado oil.
2. Make the dough: Place the mozzarella cheese and butter in a microwave-safe bowl and microwave for 1 to 2 minutes, until the cheese is entirely melted. Stir well. Add the egg and, using a hand mixer on low speed, combine well. Add the almond flour and salt and combine well with the hand mixer.
3. Lay a piece of greaseproof paper on the countertop and place the dough on it. Knead it for about 3 minutes; the dough should be thick yet pliable. (Note: If the dough is too sticky, chill it in the refrigerator for an hour or overnight.) Place the dough in the prepared casserole dish and use your hands to spread it out to fill the bottom of the casserole dish.
4. Make the garlic butter: In a small dish, stir together the butter and garlic until well combined.
5. Spread the garlic butter on top of the dough. Top with the Parmesan, basil, and oregano. Place in the air fryer and cook for 10 minutes, or until golden brown and cooked through.
6. Cut into 1-inch-wide breadsticks and serve with marinara sauce, if desired. Best served fresh, but leftovers can be stored in an airtight container in the fridge for up to 3 days. Reheat in a preheated 200°C air fryer for 3 minutes, or until the cheese is hot and bubbly.

Bruschetta

Prep time: 6 minutes | Cook time: 8 minutes | Serves 2

- 1 small tomato, diced
- 2 tablespoons chopped fresh basil leaves
- 1 teaspoon dried oregano leaves
- ¼ teaspoon fine sea salt
- 3 tablespoons unsalted butter, softened (or olive oil for dairy-free)
- 1 clove garlic, minced
- 1 recipe Hot Dog Buns, cut into twelve ½-inch-thick slices
- ¼ cup plus 2 tablespoons shredded Parmesan cheese

1. Spray the air fryer basket or wire rack with avocado oil. Preheat the air fryer to 360°F.
2. In a small bowl, stir together the tomato, basil, oregano, and salt until well combined. Set aside.
3. In another small bowl, mix together the butter and garlic. Spread the garlic butter on one side of each hot dog bun slice.
4. Place the slices in the air fryer basket or wire rack buttered side down, spaced about ⅛ inch apart. Cook for 4 minutes. Remove the slices from the air fryer, flip them so that the buttered side is up, and top each slice with 1½ tablespoons of Parmesan and a dollop of the tomato mixture.
5. Increase the air fryer temperature to 190°C and return the slices to the air fryer basket or wire rack. Cook for another 2 to 4 minutes, until the bread is crispy and the cheese is melted.
6. Serve immediately. Alternatively, stop after step 3 and store the slices of bread and the tomato mixture in separate airtight containers in the fridge for up to 5 days. When you're ready to eat, cook as instructed in steps 4 and 5

Golden Broccoli Salad

Prep time: 5 minutes | Cook time: 7 minutes | Serves 4

- 2 cups fresh broccoli florets, chopped
- 1 tablespoon olive oil
- ¼ teaspoon salt
- ⅛ teaspoon ground black pepper
- ¼ cup lemon juice, divided
- ¼ cup shredded Parmesan cheese
- ¼ cup sliced roasted almonds

1. In a large bowl, toss broccoli and olive oil together. Sprinkle with salt and pepper, then drizzle with 2 tablespoons lemon juice.
2. Place broccoli into ungreased air fryer basket or wire rack. Adjust the temperature to 180°C and set the timer for 7 minutes, shaking the air fryer basket or wire rack halfway through cooking. Broccoli will be golden on the edges when done.
3. Place broccoli into a large serving bowl and drizzle with remaining lemon juice. Sprinkle with Parmesan and almonds. Serve warm.

Air Fried Cauliflower

Prep time: 15 minutes | Cook time: 20 minutes | Serves 4

- ¼ cup olive oil
- 2 teaspoons curry powder
- ½ teaspoon salt
- ¼ teaspoon freshly ground black pepper
- 1 head cauliflower, cut into bite-size florets
- ½ red onion, sliced
- 2 tablespoons freshly chopped parsley, for garnish (optional)

1. Preheat the Air fryer to 200°C.
2. In a large bowl, combine the olive oil, curry powder, salt, and pepper. Add the cauliflower and onion. Toss gently until the vegetables are completely coated with the oil mixture. Transfer the vegetables to the air fryer basket or wire rack of the Air fryer.
3. Pausing about halfway through the cooking time to shake the air fryer basket or wire rack, air fry for 20 minutes until the cauliflower is tender and beginning to brown. Top with the parsley, if desired, before serving.

Cheesy Cauliflower Tots

Prep time: 15 minutes | Cook time: 12 minutes | Serves 16 tots

- 1 large head cauliflower
- 1 cup shredded Mozzarella cheese
- ½ cup grated Parmesan cheese
- 1 large egg
- ¼ teaspoon garlic powder
- ¼ teaspoon dried parsley
- ⅛ teaspoon onion powder

1. On the cooker, fill a large pot with 2 cups water and place a steamer in the pan. Bring water to a boil. Cut the cauliflower into florets and place on steamer basket. Cover pot with lid.
2. Allow cauliflower to steam 7 minutes until fork tender. Remove from steamer basket and place into cheesecloth or clean kitchen towel and let cool. Squeeze over sink to remove as much excess moisture as possible. The mixture will be too soft to form into tots if not all the moisture is removed. Mash with a fork to a smooth consistency.
3. Put the cauliflower into a large mixing bowl and add Mozzarella, Parmesan, egg, garlic powder, parsley, and onion powder. Stir until fully combined. The mixture should be wet but easy to mold.
4. Take 2 tablespoons of the mixture and roll into tot shape. Repeat with remaining mixture. Place into the air fryer basket or wire rack.
5. Adjust the temperature to 320°F (160°C) and set the timer for 12 minutes.
6. Turn tots halfway through the cooking time. Cauliflower tots should be golden when fully cooked. Serve warm.

Air fryer Carrots

Prep Time: 6 minutes| Cooking Time: 14 minutes| Servings: 4

- 6 large Carrots
- 1 tbsp. Oregano
- 2 tbsp. Olive oil
- ¼ cup Fresh parsley, chopped
- ½ tsp. Ground pepper
- ¼ tsp. Salt

1. Peel, wash, and slice carrots lengthwise.
2. Put in the air fryer basket or wire rack and drizzle some olive oil.
3. Set the temperature of your Air fryer at 180°C and time to 12 minutes.
4. Shake the air fryer basket or wire rack intermittently.
5. After 12 minutes, add seasoning and cook 2 minutes further at 392°F.
6. Garnish with chopped parsley and serve hot.

Cheese Cauliflower Mash

Prep time: 10 minutes | Cook time: 15 minutes | Serves 6

- 1 (12-ounce / 340-g) steamer bag cauliflower florets, cooked according to package instructions
- 2 tablespoons salted butter, softened
- 2 ounces (57 g) cream cheese, softened
- ½ cup shredded sharp Cheddar cheese
- ¼ cup pickled jalapeños
- ½ teaspoon salt
- ¼ teaspoon ground black pepper

1. Place cooked cauliflower into a food processor with remaining ingredients. Pulse twenty times until cauliflower is smooth and all ingredients are combined.
2. Spoon mash into an ungreased 6-inch round nonstick baking dish. Place dish into air fryer basket or wire rack. Adjust the temperature to 190°C and set the timer for 15 minutes. The top will be golden brown when done. Serve warm.

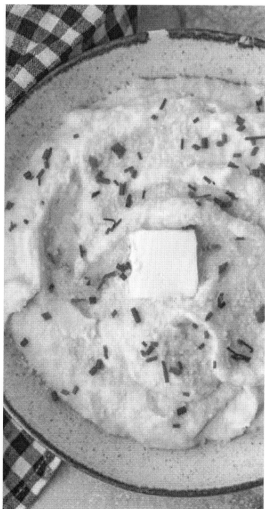

Ranch Cheddar Cauliflower Steaks

Prep time: 10 minutes | Cook time: 15 minutes | Serves 2

- 1 head cauliflower, stemmed and leaves removed
- ¼ cup rapeseed oil
- ½ teaspoon garlic powder
- ½ teaspoon paprika
- Sea salt, to taste
- Freshly ground black pepper, to taste
- 1 cup shredded Cheddar cheese
- Ranch dressing, for garnish
- 4 slices bacon, cooked and crumbled
- 2 tablespoons chopped fresh chives

1. Cut the cauliflower from top to bottom into two 2-inch "steaks"; reserve the remaining cauliflower to cook separately.
2. Insert the Grill Grate and close the hood. Select GRILL, set the temperature to MAX, and set the time to 15 minutes. Select START/STOP to begin preheating.
3. Meanwhile, in a small bowl, whisk together the oil, garlic powder, and paprika. Season with salt and pepper. Brush each steak with the oil mixture on both sides.
4. When the unit beeps to signify it has preheated, place the steaks on the Grill Grate. Close the hood and cook for 10 minutes.
5. After 10 minutes, flip the steaks and top each with ½ cup of cheese. Close the hood and continue to cook until the cheese is melted, about 5 minutes.
6. When cooking is complete, place the cauliflower steaks on a plate and drizzle with the ranch dressing. Top with the bacon and chives.

Mozzarella aubergine and Tomato Stacks

Prep time: 5 minutes | Cook time: 10 minutes | Serves 4

- 1 aubergine, sliced ¼-inch thick
- 2 tablespoons rapeseed oil
- 2 beefsteak or heirloom tomatoes, sliced ¼-inch thick
- 12 large basil leaves
- ½ pound (227 g) buffalo Mozzarella, sliced ¼-inch thick
- Sea salt, to taste

1. Insert the Grill Grate and close the hood. Select GRILL, set the temperature to MAX, and set the time to 14 minutes. Select START/STOP to begin preheating.
2. Meanwhile, in a large bowl, toss the aubergine and oil until evenly coated.
3. When the unit beeps to signify it has preheated, place the aubergine on the Grill Grate. Close the hood and grill for 8 to 12 minutes, until charred on all sides.
4. After 8 to 12 minutes, top the aubergine with one slice each of tomato and Mozzarella. Close the hood and grill for 2 minutes, until the cheese melts.
5. When cooking is complete, remove the aubergine stacks from the grill. Place 2 or 3 basil leaves on top of half of the stacks. Place the remaining aubergine stacks on top of those with basil so that there are four stacks total. Season with salt, garnish with the remaining basil, and serve.

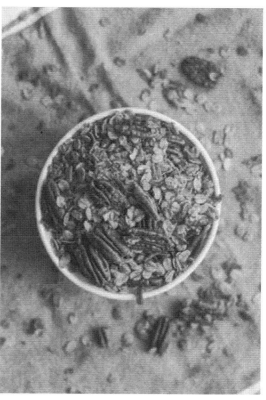

Herbed Broccoli with Cheese

Prep time: 5 minutes | Cook time: 18 minutes | Serves 4

- 1 large-sized head broccoli, stemmed and cut into small florets
- 2½ tablespoons rapeseed oil
- 2 teaspoons dried basil
- 2 teaspoons dried rosemary
- Salt and ground black pepper, to taste
- ⅓ cup grated yellow cheese

1. Bring a pot of lightly salted water to a boil. Add the broccoli florets to the boiling water and let boil for about 3 minutes.
2. Drain the broccoli florets well and transfer to a large bowl. Add the rapeseed oil, basil, rosemary, salt, and black pepper to the bowl and toss until the broccoli is fully coated. Place the broccoli in the air fry basket.
3. Select Air Fry, set temperature to 200°C, and set time to 15 minutes. Select Start/Stop to begin preheating.
4. Once preheated, place the air fry basket on the air fry position. Stir the broccoli halfway through the cooking time.
5. When cooking is complete, the broccoli should be crisp. Remove the air fryer basket or wire rack from the oven. Serve the broccoli warm with grated cheese sprinkled on top.

Broccoli and rocket Cheese Salad

Prep time: 15 minutes | Cook time: 8 minutes | Serves 4

- 2 heads broccoli, trimmed into florets
- ½ red onion, sliced
- 1 tablespoon rapeseed oil
- 2 tablespoons extra-virgin olive oil
- 1 tablespoon freshly squeezed lemon juice
- 1 teaspoon honey
- 1 teaspoon Dijon mustard
- 1 garlic clove, minced
- Pinch red pepper flakes
- ¼ teaspoon fine sea salt
- Freshly ground black pepper, to taste
- 4 cups rocket, torn
- 2 tablespoons grated Parmesan cheese

1. Insert the Grill Grate and close the hood. Select GRILL, set the temperature to MAX, and set the time to 12 minutes. Select START/STOP to begin preheating.
2. While the unit is preheating, in a large bowl, combine the broccoli, sliced onions, and rapeseed oil and toss until coated.
3. When the unit beeps to signify it has preheated, place the vegetables on the Grill Grate. Close the hood and grill for 8 to 12 minutes, until charred on all sides.
4. Meanwhile, in a medium bowl, whisk together the olive oil, lemon juice, honey, mustard, garlic, red pepper flakes, salt, and pepper.
5. When cooking is complete, combine the roasted vegetables and rocket in a large serving bowl. Drizzle with the vinaigrette to taste, and sprinkle with the Parmesan cheese.

Maple and Pecan muesli

Prep time: 5 minutes | Cook time: 20 minutes | Serves 4

- 1½ cups rolled oats
- ¼ cup maple syrup
- ¼ cup pecan pieces
- 1 teaspoon vanilla extract
- ½ teaspoon ground cinnamon

1. Line a baking tray with greaseproof paper.
2. Mix together the oats, maple syrup, pecan pieces, vanilla, and cinnamon in a large bowl and stir until the oats and pecan pieces are completely coated. Spread the mixture evenly on the baking tray.
3. Select Bake, set temperature to 150°C , and set time to 20 minutes. Select Start/Stop to begin preheating.
4. Once preheated, place the baking tray on the bake position. Stir once halfway through the cooking time.
5. When done, remove from the oven and cool for 30 minutes before serving. The muesli may still be a bit soft right after removing, but it will gradually firm up as it cools.

Caramelized aubergine with Yogurt Sauce

Prep time: 5 minutes | Cook time: 15 minutes | Serves 2

- 1 medium aubergine, quartered and cut crosswise into ½-inch-thick slices
- 2 tablespoons vegetable oil
- flake salt and freshly ground black pepper, to taste
- ½ cup plain yogurt (not Greek)
- 2 tablespoons harissa paste
- 1 garlic clove, grated
- 2 teaspoons honey

1. Toss the aubergine slices with the vegetable oil, salt, and pepper in a large bowl until well coated.
2. Lay the aubergine slices in the air fry basket.
3. Select Air Fry, set temperature to 200°C, and set time to 15 minutes. Select Start/Stop to begin preheating.
4. Once preheated, place the air fry basket on the air fry position. Stir the slices two to three times during cooking.
5. Meanwhile, make the yogurt sauce by whisking together the yogurt, harissa paste, and garlic in a small bowl.
6. When cooking is complete, the aubergine slices should be golden brown. Spread the yogurt sauce on a platter, and pile the aubergine slices over the top. Serve drizzled with the honey.

Bean, Salsa, and Cheese Tacos

Prep time: 12 minutes | Cook time: 7 minutes | Serves 4

- 1 (15-ounce / 425-g) can black beans, drained and rinsed
- ½ cup prepared salsa
- 1½ teaspoons chili powder
- 4 ounces (113 g) grated Parmesan Cheese
- 2 tablespoons minced onion
- 8 (6-inch) flour tortillas
- 2 tablespoons vegetable or extra-virgin olive oil
- Shredded lettuce, for serving

1. In a medium bowl, add the beans, salsa and chili powder. Coarsely mash them with a potato masher. Fold in the cheese and onion and stir until combined.
2. Arrange the flour tortillas on a cutting board and spoon 2 to 3 tablespoons of the filling into each tortilla. Fold the tortillas over, pressing lightly to even out the filling. Brush the tacos on one side with half the olive oil and put them, oiled side down, on the sheet pan. Brush the top side with the remaining olive oil.
3. Select Air Fry, set temperature to 200°C, and set time to 7 minutes. Select Start/Stop to begin preheating.
4. Once preheated, place the pan into the oven. Flip the tacos halfway through the cooking time.
5. Remove the pan from the oven and allow to cool for 5 minutes. Serve with the shredded lettuce on the side.

Mushroom, Tomato and Microgreens Buds

Prep time: 10 minutes | Cook time: 8 minutes | Serves 4

- 8 small portobello mushrooms, trimmed with gills removed
- 2 tablespoons rapeseed oil
- 2 tablespoons balsamic vinegar
- 8 slider buns
- 1 tomato, sliced
- ½ cup pesto
- ½ cup microgreens

1. Insert the Grill Grate and close the hood. Select GRILL, set the temperature to HIGH, and set the time to 8 minutes. Select START/STOP to begin preheating.
2. While the unit is preheating, brush the mushrooms with the oil and balsamic vinegar.
3. When the unit beeps to signify it has preheated, place the mushrooms, gill-side down, on the Grill Grate. Close the hood and grill for 8 minutes, until the mushrooms are tender.
4. When cooking is complete, remove the mushrooms from the grill, and layer on the buns with tomato, pesto, and microgreens.

Easy Cheesy Vegetable Quesadilla

Prep time: 5 minutes | Cook time: 10 minutes | Serves 1

- 1 teaspoon olive oil
- 2 flour tortillas
- ¼ courgette, sliced
- ¼ yellow bell pepper, sliced
- ¼ cup shredded gouda cheese
- 1 tablespoon chopped Coriander
- ½ green onion, sliced

1. Coat the air fry basket with 1 teaspoon of olive oil.
2. Arrange a flour tortilla in the air fry basket and scatter the top with courgette, bell pepper, gouda cheese, Coriander, and green onion. Place the other flour tortilla on top.
3. Select Air Fry, set temperature to 200°C, and set time to 10 minutes. Select Start/Stop to begin preheating.
4. Once preheated, place the air fryer basket or wire rack on the air fry position.
5. When cooking is complete, the tortillas should be lightly browned and the vegetables should be tender. Remove from the oven and cool for 5 minutes before slicing into wedges.

Cayenne Tahini Kale

Prep time: 5 minutes | Cook time: 15 minutes | Serves 2 to 4

DRESSING:
- ¼ cup tahini
- ¼ cup fresh lemon juice
- 2 tablespoons olive oil
- 1 teaspoon sesame seeds
- ½ teaspoon garlic powder
- ¼ teaspoon cayenne pepper

KALE:
- 4 cups packed torn kale leaves (stems and ribs removed and leaves torn into palm-size pieces)
- flake salt and freshly ground black pepper, to taste

1. Make the dressing: Whisk together the tahini, lemon juice, olive oil, sesame seeds, garlic powder, and cayenne pepper in a large bowl until well mixed.
2. Add the kale and massage the dressing thoroughly all over the leaves. Sprinkle the salt and pepper to season.
3. Place the kale in the air fry basket in a single layer.
4. Select Air Fry, set temperature to 180°C, and set time to 15 minutes. Select Start/Stop to begin preheating.
5. Once preheated, place the air fry basket on the air fry position.
6. When cooking is complete, the leaves should be slightly wilted and crispy. Remove from the oven and serve on a plate.

Southwest Stuffed Bell Peppers

Prep time: 15 minutes | Cook time: 32 minutes | Serves 6

- 6 red or green bell peppers, seeded, ribs removed, and top ½-inch cut off and reserved
- 4 garlic cloves, minced
- 1 small white onion, diced
- 2 (8½-ounce / 241-g) bags instant rice, cooked in microwave
- 1 (10-ounce / 283-g) can red or green enchilada sauce
- ½ teaspoon chili powder
- ¼ teaspoon ground cumin
- ½ cup tinned black beans, rinsed and drained
- ½ cup frozen corn
- ½ cup vegetable stock
- 1 (8-ounce / 227-g) bag shredded Colby Jack cheese, divided

1. Chop the ½-inch portions of reserved bell pepper and place in a large mixing bowl. Add the garlic, onion, cooked instant rice, enchilada sauce, chili powder, cumin, black beans, corn, vegetable stock, and half the cheese. Mix to combine.
2. Use the cooking pot without the Grill Grate or Crisper Basket installed. Close the hood. Select ROAST, set the temperature to 180°C, and set the time to 32 minutes. Select START/STOP to begin preheating.
3. While the unit is preheating, spoon the mixture into the peppers, filling them up as full as possible. If necessary, lightly press the mixture down into the peppers to fit more in.
4. When the unit beeps to signify it has preheated, place the peppers, upright, in the pot. Close the hood and cook for 30 minutes.
5. After 30 minutes, sprinkle the remaining cheese over the top of the peppers. Close the hood and cook for the remaining 2 minutes.
6. When cooking is complete, serve immediately.

Sweet and Spicy Broccoli

Prep time: 10 minutes | Cook time: 15 to 20 minutes | Serves 4

- ½ teaspoon olive oil, plus more for greasing
- 1 pound (454 g) fresh broccoli, cut into florets
- ½ tablespoon minced garlic
- Salt, to taste
- Sauce:
- 1½ tablespoons soy sauce
- 2 teaspoons chili sauce or sriracha
- 1½ teaspoons honey
- 1 teaspoon white vinegar
- Freshly ground black pepper, to taste

1. Grease the air fry basket with olive oil.
2. Add the broccoli florets, ½ teaspoon of olive oil, and garlic to a large bowl and toss well. Season with salt to taste.
3. Put the broccoli in the air fry basket in a single layer.
4. Select Air Fry, set temperature to 200°C, and set time to 15 minutes. Select Start/Stop to begin preheating.
5. Once preheated, place the air fry basket on the air fry position. Stir the broccoli florets three times during cooking.
6. Meanwhile, whisk together all the ingredients for the sauce in a small bowl until well incorporated. If the honey doesn't incorporate well, microwave the sauce for 10 to 20 seconds until the honey is melted.
7. When cooking is complete, the broccoli should be lightly browned and crispy. Continue cooking for 5 minutes, if desired. Remove from the oven to a serving bowl. Pour over the sauce and toss to combine. Add more salt and pepper, if needed. Serve warm.

Grilled Vegetable Pizza

Prep time: 10 minutes | Cook time: 10 minutes | Serves 2

- 2 tablespoons plain flour, plus more as needed
- ½ store-bought pizza dough (about 8 ounces / 227 g)
- 1 tablespoon rapeseed oil, divided
- ½ cup pizza sauce
- 1 cup shredded Mozzarella cheese
- ½ courgette, thinly sliced
- ½ red onion, sliced
- ½ red bell pepper, seeded and thinly sliced

1. Place the grill plate on the grill position. Select Grill, set the temperature to 200°C, and set the time to 7 minutes.
2. Dust a clean work surface with the flour.
3. Place the dough on the floured surface and roll it into a 9-inch round of even thickness. Dust your rolling pin and work surface with additional flour, as needed, to ensure the dough does not stick.
4. Evenly brush the surface of the rolled-out dough with ½ tablespoon of oil. Flip the dough over and brush the other side with the remaining ½ tablespoon of oil. Poke the dough with a fork 5 or 6 times across its surface to prevent air pockets from forming while it cooks.
5. Place the dough on the grill plate. Grill for 4 minutes.
6. After 4 minutes, flip the dough, then spread the pizza sauce evenly over it. Sprinkle with the cheese, and top with the courgette, onion, and pepper.
7. Continue cooking for the remaining 2 to 3 minutes until the cheese is melted and the veggie slices begin to crisp.
8. When cooking is complete, let cool slightly before slicing.

Rocket and Broccoli Salad

Prep time: 10 minutes | Cook time: 12 minutes | Serves 4

- 2 heads broccoli, trimmed into florets
- ½ red onion, sliced
- 1 tablespoon rapeseed oil
- 2 tablespoons extra-virgin olive oil
- 1 tablespoon freshly squeezed lemon juice
- 1 teaspoon honey
- 1 teaspoon Dijon mustard
- 1 garlic clove, minced
- Pinch red pepper flakes
- ¼ teaspoon fine sea salt
- Freshly ground black pepper, to taste
- 4 cups rocket, torn
- 2 tablespoons grated Parmesan cheese

1. Place the grill plate on the grill position. Select Grill, set the temperature to 200°C, and set the time to 12 minutes.
2. In a large bowl, combine the broccoli, sliced onions, and rapeseed oil and toss until coated.
3. Place the vegetables on the grill plate. Grill for 8 to 12 minutes, until charred on all sides.
4. Meanwhile, in a medium bowl, whisk together the olive oil, lemon juice, honey, mustard, garlic, red pepper flakes, salt, and pepper.
5. When cooking is complete, combine the roasted vegetables and rocket in a large serving bowl. Drizzle with the vinaigrette, and sprinkle with the Parmesan cheese.

Summer marrow and courgette Salad

Prep time: 10 minutes | Cook time: 20 minutes | Serves 4

- 1 courgette, sliced lengthwise about ¼-inch thick
- 1 summer marrow, sliced lengthwise about ¼-inch thick
- ½ red onion, sliced
- 4 tablespoons rapeseed oil, divided
- 2 portobello mushroom caps, trimmed with gills removed
- 2 ears corn, hulled
- 2 teaspoons freshly squeezed lemon juice
- Sea salt, to taste
- Freshly ground black pepper, to taste

1. Place the grill plate on the grill position. Select Grill, set the temperature to 200°C, and set the time to 25 minutes.
2. Meanwhile, in a large bowl, toss the courgette, marrow, and onion with 2 tablespoons of oil until evenly coated.
3. Arrange the courgette, marrow, and onions on the grill plate. Grill for 6 minutes.
4. After 6 minutes, flip the marrow. Grill for 6 to 9 minutes more.
5. Meanwhile, brush the mushrooms and corn with the remaining 2 tablespoons of oil.
6. When cooking is complete, remove the courgette, marrow, and onions and swap in the mushrooms and corn. Grill for the remaining 10 minutes.
7. When cooking is complete, remove the mushrooms and corn, and let cool.
8. Cut the kernels from the cobs. Roughly chop all the vegetables into bite-size pieces.
9. Place the vegetables in a serving bowl and drizzle with lemon juice. Season with salt and pepper, and toss until evenly mixed.

Bean and Corn Stuffed Peppers

Prep time: 15 minutes | Cook time: 32 minutes | Serves 6

- 6 red or green bell peppers, seeded, ribs removed, and top ½-inch cut off and reserved
- 4 garlic cloves, minced
- 1 small white onion, diced
- 2 (8½-ounce / 241-g) bags instant rice, cooked in microwave
- 1 (10-ounce / 284-g) can red or green enchilada sauce
- ½ teaspoon chili powder
- ¼ teaspoon ground cumin
- ½ cup tinned black beans, rinsed and drained
- ½ cup frozen corn
- ½ cup vegetable stock
- 1 (8-ounce / 227-g) bag shredded Colby Jack cheese, divided

1. Chop the ½-inch portions of reserved bell pepper and place in a large mixing bowl. Add the garlic, onion, cooked instant rice, enchilada sauce, chili powder, cumin, black beans, corn, vegetable stock, and half the cheese. Mix to combine.
2. Place the baking pan on the roast position. Select Roast, set the temperature to 180°C, and set the time to 32 minutes.
3. Spoon the mixture into the peppers, filling them up as full as possible. If necessary, lightly press the mixture down into the peppers to fit more in.
4. Place the peppers, upright, in the pan. Roast for 30 minutes.
5. After 30 minutes, sprinkle the remaining cheese over the top of the peppers. Roast for the remaining 2 minutes.
6. When cooking is complete, serve immediately.

Cauliflower Steaks with Ranch Dressing

Prep time: 10 minutes | Cook time: 15 minutes | Serves 2

- 1 head cauliflower, stemmed and leaves removed
- ¼ cup rapeseed oil
- ½ teaspoon garlic powder
- ½ teaspoon paprika
- Sea salt, to taste
- Freshly ground black pepper, to taste
- 1 cup shredded Cheddar cheese
- Ranch dressing, for garnish
- 4 slices bacon, cooked and crumbled
- 2 tablespoons chopped fresh chives

1. Cut the cauliflower from top to bottom into two 2-inch "steaks"; reserve the remaining cauliflower to cook separately.
2. Place the grill plate on the grill position. Select Grill, set the temperature to 200°C, and set the time to 15 minutes.
3. Meanwhile, in a small bowl, whisk together the oil, garlic powder, and paprika. Season with salt and pepper. Brush each steak with the oil mixture on both sides.
4. Place the steaks on the grill plate. Grill for 10 minutes.
5. After 10 minutes, flip the steaks and top each with ½ cup of cheese. Continue to grill until the cheese is melted, about 5 minutes.
6. When cooking is complete, place the cauliflower steaks on a plate and drizzle with the ranch dressing. Top with the bacon and chives.

Chapter 9
Starters and Snacks

Ham and Cheese Stuffed Peppers

Prep time: 5 minutes | Cook time: 7 minutes | Serves 4

- 8 Serrano peppers
- 4 ounces (113 g) ham cubes
- 4 ounces (113 g) goat cheese, crumbled

1. Start by preheating the air fryer to 190°C.
2. Stuff the peppers with ham and cheese; transfer them to a lightly oiled crisper tray.
3. Place the crisper tray in the corresponding position in the air fryer. Select Air Fry and cook the peppers for about 7 minutes or until golden brown.
4. Bon appétit!

Cheese Stuffed Mushrooms

Prep time: 10 minutes | Cook time: 7 minutes | Serves 4

- 1 tablespoon butter
- 6 ounces (170 g) Pecorino Romano cheese, grated
- 2 tablespoons chopped chives
- 1 tablespoon minced garlic
- ½ teaspoon cayenne pepper
- Sea salt and ground black pepper, to taste
- 1 pound (454 g) button mushrooms, stems removed

1. Start by preheating the air fryer to 200°C.
2. In a mixing bowl, thoroughly combine the butter, cheese, chives, garlic, cayenne pepper, salt, and black pepper.
3. Divide the filling between the mushrooms. Arrange the mushrooms in the crisper tray.
4. Place the crisper tray in the corresponding position in the air fryer. Select Air Fry and cook the mushrooms for about 7 minutes, shaking the crisper tray halfway through the cooking time.
5. Bon appétit!

Veggie Prawn Toast

Prep time: 15 minutes | Cook time: 6 minutes | Serves 4

- 8 large raw Prawn, peeled and finely chopped
- 1 egg white
- 2 garlic cloves, minced
- 3 tablespoons minced red bell pepper
- 1 medium celery stalk, minced
- 2 tablespoons cornflour
- ¼ teaspoon Chinese five-spice powder
- 3 slices firm thin-sliced no-sodium whole-wheat bread

1. Preheat the air fryer oven to 180°C.
2. In a small bowl, stir together the Prawn, egg white, garlic, red bell pepper, celery, cornflour, and five-spice powder. Top each slice of bread with one-third of the Prawn mixture, spreading it evenly to the edges. With a sharp knife, cut each slice of bread into 4 strips.
3. Place the Prawn toasts in the air fryer basket or wire rack in a single layer.
4. Place the air fryer basket or wire rack onto the baking pan, select Air Fry and set time to 6 minutes, or until crisp and golden brown.
5. Serve hot.

Pasta Chips

Prep time: 7 minutes | Cook time: 10 minutes | Serves 4

- 2 cups (152 g) dry whole wheat bow tie pasta (use brown rice pasta)
- 1 tablespoon (15 ml) olive oil (or use aquafaba)
- 1 tablespoon (7 g) nutritional yeast
- 1½ teaspoon (3 g) italian seasoning blend
- ½ teaspoon salt

1. Cook the pasta according to your package directions with the important exception of only cooking it for half the time listed, then drain the pasta well.
2. Toss the drained pasta with the olive oil (or aquafaba), nutritional yeast, italian seasoning blend and salt.
3. Place about half of the mixture in your air fryer basket or wire rack if yours is small; larger ones may be able to cook in one batch. Cook on 200°C (200°C) for 5 minutes. Shake the air fryer basket or wire rack and cook 3 to 5 minutes more or until crunchy.

Breaded Green Tomatoes with Horseradish

Prep time: 15 minutes | Cook time: 13 minutes | Serves 4

- 2 eggs
- ¼ cup buttermilk
- ½ cup bread crumbs
- ½ cup cornmeal
- ¼ teaspoon salt
- 1½ pounds (680 g) firm green tomatoes, cut into ¼-inch slices
- Cooking spray
- Horseradish Sauce:
- ¼ cup Soured cream
- ¼ cup mayonnaise
- 2 teaspoons prepared horseradish
- ½ teaspoon lemon juice
- ½ teaspoon Worcestershire sauce
- ⅛ teaspoon black pepper

1. Spritz the air fry basket with cooking spray. Set aside.
2. In a small bowl, whisk together all the ingredients for the horseradish sauce until smooth. Set aside.
3. In a shallow dish, beat the eggs and buttermilk.
4. In a separate shallow dish, thoroughly combine the bread crumbs, cornmeal, and salt.
5. Dredge the tomato slices, one at a time, in the egg mixture, then roll in the bread crumb mixture until evenly coated.
6. Place the tomato slices in the air fry basket in a single layer. Spray them with cooking spray.
7. Select Air Fry, set temperature to 200°C, and set time to 13 minutes. Select Start/Stop to begin preheating.
8. Once preheated, place the air fryer basket or wire rack on the air fry position. Flip the tomato slices halfway through the cooking time.
9. When cooking is complete, the tomato slices should be nicely browned and crisp. Remove from the oven to a platter and serve drizzled with the prepared horseradish sauce.

Spicy Corn Tortilla Chips

Prep time: 5 minutes | Cook time: 5 minutes | Serves 4

- ½ teaspoon ground cumin
- ½ teaspoon paprika
- ½ teaspoon chili powder
- ½ teaspoon salt
- Pinch cayenne pepper
- 8 (6-inch) corn tortillas, each cut into 6 wedges
- Cooking spray

1. Lightly spritz the air fry basket with cooking spray.
2. Stir together the cumin, paprika, chili powder, salt, and pepper in a small bowl.
3. Place the tortilla wedges in the air fry basket in a single layer. Lightly mist them with cooking spray. Sprinkle the seasoning mixture on top of the tortilla wedges.
4. Select Air Fry, set temperature to 190°C, and set time to 5 minutes. Select Start/Stop to begin preheating.
5. Once preheated, place the air fryer basket or wire rack on the air fry position. Stir the tortilla wedges halfway through the cooking time.
6. When cooking is complete, the chips should be lightly browned and crunchy. Remove the air fryer basket or wire rack from the oven. Let the tortilla chips cool for 5 minutes and serve.

Hush Puppies

Prep time: 7 minutes | Cook time: 20 minutes | Serves 2

- ¼ cup plus 2 tablespoons plain flour
- ½ cup yellow cornmeal
- 2 tablespoons dried minced onion
- ¾ teaspoon baking powder
- ⅛ teaspoon granulated sugar
- ¼ teaspoon salt
- 1 egg
- ¼ cup plus 2 tablespoons milk
- Cooking spray

1. Preheat the air fryer to 180°C.
2. In a large bowl, combine the flour, cornmeal, dried minced onion, baking powder, sugar, and salt. Whisk in the egg and the milk.
3. Divide and roll the mixture into tablespoon-size into balls.
4. Place the balls in the air fryer basket or wire rack, and spritz with cooking spray. Air fry for 20 minutes or until golden brown. Flip the balls halfway through.
5. Serve hot.

Hot Chickpeas

Prep time: 5 minutes | Cook time: 18 minutes | Serves 4

- ½ teaspoon chili powder
- ½ teaspoon ground cumin
- ¼ teaspoon cayenne pepper
- ¼ teaspoon salt
- 1 (19-ounce / 539-g) can chickpeas, drained and rinsed
- Cooking spray

1. Lina the air fry basket with greaseproof paper and lightly spritz with cooking spray.
2. Mix the chili powder, cumin, cayenne pepper, and salt in a small bowl.
3. Place the chickpeas in a medium bowl and lightly mist with cooking spray.
4. Add the spice mixture to the chickpeas and toss until evenly coated. Transfer the chickpeas to the parchment.
5. Select Air Fry, set temperature to 200°C, and set time to 18 minutes. Select Start/Stop to begin preheating.
6. Once preheated, place the air fryer basket or wire rack on the air fry position. Stir the chickpeas twice during cooking.
7. When cooking is complete, the chickpeas should be crunchy. Remove the air fryer basket or wire rack from the oven. Let the chickpeas cool for 5 minutes before serving.

Chile Chicken Drumettes

Prep time: 5 minutes | Cook time: 18 minutes | Serves 5

- 2 pounds (907 g) chicken drumettes
- 1 teaspoon ancho chile pepper
- 1 teaspoon smoked paprika
- 1 teaspoon onion powder
- 1 teaspoon garlic powder
- flake salt and ground black pepper, to taste
- ¼ tsp black pepper
- 2 tablespoons olive oil

1. Start by preheating the air fryer to 190°C.
2. Toss the chicken drumettes with the remaining ingredients. Transfer to the crisper tray.
3. Place the crisper tray in the corresponding position in the air fryer. Select Roast and cook the chicken drumettes for 18 minutes, turning them over halfway through the cooking time.
4. Bon appétit!

Cauliflower with Cheese

Prep time: 5 minutes | Cook time: 15 minutes | Serves 4

- ½ cup milk
- 1 cup plain flour
- 1 teaspoon garlic powder
- 1 teaspoon onion powder
- 1 teaspoon hot paprika
- Sea salt and ground black pepper, to taste
- 2 tablespoons olive oil
- 1 pound (454 g) cauliflower florets
- 4 ounces (113 g) Parmesan cheese, preferably freshly grated

1. Start by preheating the air fryer to 180°C.
2. In a mixing bowl, thoroughly combine the milk, flour, spices, and olive oil.
3. Dip the cauliflower florets in the flour mixture. Transfer to the crisper tray.
4. Place the crisper tray in the corresponding position in the air fryer. Select Air Fry and cook the cauliflower florets for about 10 minutes, turning them over halfway through the cooking time.
5. Top the cauliflower florets with cheese and continue to cook an additional 5 minutes.
6. Bon appétit!

Cheesy Broccoli Bites

Prep time: 5 minutes | Cook time: 10 minutes | Serves 4

- 1 pound (454 g) broccoli florets
- 1 teaspoon granulated garlic
- 1 tablespoon dried onion flakes
- 1 teaspoon crushed red pepper flakes
- 2 tablespoons olive oil
- ½ cup grated Pecorino Romano cheese

1. Start by preheating the air fryer to 190°C.
2. Toss all ingredients in a lightly oiled crisper tray.
3. Place the crisper tray in the corresponding position in the air fryer. Select Air Fry and cook the broccoli florets for about 10 minutes, shaking the crisper tray halfway through the cooking time.
4. Enjoy!

Brussels Sprouts with Cheese

Prep time: 10 minutes | Cook time: 10 minutes | Serves 4

- 1 pound (454 g) Brussels sprouts, trimmed
- 2 tablespoons butter, melted
- Sea salt and freshly ground black pepper, to taste
- 1 teaspoon minced garlic
- 2 tablespoons red wine vinegar
- 2 ounces (57 g) Cheddar cheese, shredded

1. Start by preheating the air fryer to 190°C.
2. Toss the Brussels sprouts with the remaining ingredients; then, arrange the Brussels sprouts in the crisper tray.
3. Place the crisper tray in the corresponding position in the air fryer. Select Air Fry and cook the Brussels sprouts for 10 minutes, shaking the crisper tray halfway through the cooking time.
4. Serve warm and enjoy!

Chile Pork Ribs

Prep time: 5 minutes | Cook time: 35 minutes | Serves 4

- 1½ pounds (680 g) spare ribs
- flake salt and ground black pepper, to taste
- 2 teaspoons Demerara sugar
- 1 teaspoon paprika
- 1 teaspoon chile powder
- 1 teaspoon garlic powder

1. Start by preheating the air fryer to 180°C.
2. Toss all the ingredients in a lightly greased crisper tray.
3. Place the crisper tray in the corresponding position in the air fryer. Select Air Fry and cook the pork ribs for 35 minutes, turning them over halfway through the cooking time.
4. Bon appétit!

Carrot with Butter

Prep time: 5 minutes | Cook time: 15 minutes | Serves 4

- 1 pound (454 g) baby carrots
- 2 tablespoons butter
- flake salt and ground white pepper, to taste
- 1 teaspoon paprika
- 1 teaspoon dried oregano

1. Start by preheating the air fryer to 190°C.
2. Toss the carrots with the remaining ingredients; then, arrange the carrots in the crisper tray.
3. Place the crisper tray in the corresponding position in the air fryer. Select Air Fry and cook the carrots for 15 minutes, shaking the crisper tray halfway through the cooking time.
4. Bon appétit!

Syrupy Chicken Wings

Prep time: 6 minutes | Cook time: 18 minutes | Serves 5

- 2 pounds (907 g) chicken wings
- ¼ cup agave syrup
- 2 tablespoons soy sauce
- 2 tablespoons chopped scallions
- 2 tablespoons olive oil
- 1 teaspoon peeled and grated ginger
- 2 cloves garlic, minced
- Sea salt and ground black pepper, to taste

1. Start by preheating the air fryer to 190°C.
2. Toss the chicken wings with the remaining ingredients. Transfer to the crisper tray.
3. Place the crisper tray in the corresponding position in the air fryer. Select Roast and cook the chicken wings for 18 minutes, turning them over halfway through the cooking time.
4. Bon appétit!

Creamy Mushroom Cheese Frittata

Prep time: 6 minutes | Cook time: 15 minutes | Serves 3

- 6 eggs
- ¼ cup Soured cream
- ½ cup shredded Emmethaler
- flake salt and ground black pepper, to taste
- 1 teaspoon hot paprika
- 2 tablespoons olive oil
- 2 cloves garlic, crushed
- 6 ounces (170 g) brown mushrooms, sliced
- 2 tablespoons roughly chopped fresh parsley

1. Start by preheating the air fryer to 180°C.
2. Spritz the sides and bottom of the baking pan with nonstick cooking oil.
3. In a mixing bowl, thoroughly combine all the ingredients.
4. Pour the mixture into the prepared baking pan.
5. Place the baking pan in the corresponding position in the air fryer. Select Bake and cook the frittata for approximately 15 minutes, or until a toothpick comes out dry and clean.
6. Bon appétit!

Potato Cheese Sticks

Prep time: 6 minutes | Cook time: 14 minutes | Serves 4

- 1 cup mashed boiled potato
- 1 cup grated Cheddar cheese
- 1 tablespoon miso paste
- 1 cup plain flour
- ½ teaspoon coriander seeds
- Sea salt and ground black pepper, to taste
- 1 egg, beaten
- 1 cup bread crumbs
- 2 tablespoons Kewpie Japanese mayonnaise

1. Start by preheating the air fryer to 200°C.
2. Mix all the ingredients, except for the bread crumbs, in a bowl. Press the mixture into a parchment-lined baking pan and allow it to freeze until firm.
3. Cut the mixture into sticks and roll them into the bread crumbs; place the sticks in a lightly oiled crisper tray.
4. Place the crisper tray in the corresponding position in the air fryer. Select Air Fry and cook the sticks for about 14 minutes, shaking the crisper tray halfway through the cooking time.
5. Bon appétit!

Pork and Turkey Cheese Meatballs

Prep time: 5 minutes | Cook time: 15 minutes | Serves 4

- ½ pound (227 g) ground pork
- ½ pound (227 g) ground turkey
- 1 onion, minced
- 2 garlic cloves, minced
- ¼ cup Italian-style bread crumbs
- ¼ cup grated Parmesan cheese
- 1 large-sized egg, whisked
- Sea salt and ground black pepper, to taste

1. Start by preheating the air fryer to 190°C.
2. Mix all the ingredients until everything is well combined. Form the mixture into balls. Transfer to the crisper tray.
3. Place the crisper tray in the corresponding position in the air fryer. Select Air Fry and cook the meatballs for about 15 minutes or until cooked through, shaking the crisper tray halfway through the cooking time.
4. Bon appétit!

Eggs Salad with Yogurt

Prep time: 5 minutes | Cook time: 15 minutes | Serves 4

- 6 eggs
- 4 tablespoons Greek-style yogurt
- 4 tablespoons mayonnaise
- 3 tablespoons chopped scallions
- 1 tablespoon Dijon mustard
- Sea salt and ground black pepper, to taste

1. Start by preheating the air fryer to 270°F (132°C).
2. Place the eggs in the crisper tray.
3. Place the crisper tray in the corresponding position in the air fryer. Select Air Fry and cook the eggs for about 15 minutes.
4. Peel and chop the eggs; place them in a salad bowl and add in the remaining ingredients. Gently toss to combine.
5. Place the salad in the refrigerator until ready to serve. Bon appétit!

Eggs Muffins with Bacon

Prep time: 6 minutes | Cook time: 15 minutes | Serves 4

- 6 eggs
- 6 tablespoons crumbled cottage cheese
- 2 tablespoons chopped scallions
- 1 teaspoon minced garlic
- 3 ounces (85 g) bacon, chopped
- 1 teaspoon paprika
- Sea salt and ground black pepper, to taste

1. Start by preheating the air fryer to 180°C.
2. Spritz the silicone molds with nonstick cooking oil.
3. In a mixing bowl, thoroughly combine all the ingredients.
4. Pour the mixture into the prepared silicone molds and lower them into the baking pan.
5. Place the baking pan in the corresponding position in the air fryer. Select Bake and cook the egg muffins for approximately 15 minutes, or until a toothpick comes out dry and clean.
6. Bon appétit!

Chili Chickpeas

Prep time: 5 minutes | Cook time: 13 minutes | Serves 4

- 10 ounces (283 g) chickpeas, drained and rinsed
- 1 tablespoon olive oil
- Coarse sea salt and ground black pepper, to taste
- ½ teaspoon garlic powder
- 1 teaspoon cayenne pepper
- ½ teaspoon red chili powder

1. Start by preheating the air fryer to 200°C.
2. Toss the chickpeas with the other ingredients in the crisper tray.
3. Place the crisper tray in the corresponding position in the air fryer. Select Air Fry and cook the chickpeas for about 13 minutes, tossing the crisper tray a couple of times.
4. Bon appétit!

Tofu Bowl with Pepper

Prep time: 10 minutes | Cook time: 20 minutes | Serves 4

- 2 bell peppers, sliced
- 12 ounces (340 g) firm tofu, pressed and cut into bite-sized cubes
- 2 tablespoons tamari sauce
- 2 tablespoons rice wine
- 2 tablespoons sesame oil
- 1 chili pepper, minced
- 1 garlic clove, minced

1. Start by preheating the air fryer to 200°C.
2. Toss the peppers and tofu with the remaining ingredients in the crisper tray.
3. Place the crisper tray in the corresponding position in the air fryer. Select Air Fry and cook the peppers for about 10 minutes, shaking the crisper tray halfway through the cooking time.
4. Add in the tofu cubes. Reduce the temperature to 180°C . Place the crisper tray in the corresponding position in the air fryer. Select Air Fry and cook for approximately 10 minutes.
5. Bon appétit!

Lentils and Carrot Burgers

Prep time: 8 minutes | Cook time: 15 minutes | Serves 4

- 12 ounces (340 g) tinned lentils, drained and rinsed
- 1 medium carrot, grated
- 1 medium onion, grated
- 1 garlic clove, minced
- 1 teaspoon smoked paprika
- Sea salt and ground black pepper, to taste
- 2 tablespoons olive oil

1. Start by preheating the air fryer to 190°C.
2. Mix all the ingredients until everything is well combined. Form the mixture into four patties and arrange them in a lightly greased crisper tray.
3. Place the crisper tray in the corresponding position in the air fryer. Select Air Fry and cook the burgers for about 15 minutes or until cooked through. Tun them over halfway through the cooking time.
4. Bon appétit!

Beef Cheese Sandwich

Prep time: 5 minutes | Cook time: 10 minutes | Serves 2

- 4 slices sourdough bread
- 2 tablespoons butter, room temperature
- 4 slices Cheddar cheese
- ½ pound (227 g) corned beef

1. Start by preheating the air fryer to 190°C.
2. Butter one side of each slice of bread.
3. Assemble the sandwiches with cheese and corned beef. Transfer to the crisper tray.
4. Place the crisper tray in the corresponding position in the air fryer. Select Air Fry and cook the sandwiches for about 10 minutes.
5. Bon appétit!

Cauliflower Salad

Prep time: 5 minutes | Cook time: 13 minutes | Serves 4

- 1 pound (454 g) cauliflower florets
- Sea salt and ground black pepper, to taste
- 4 tablespoons freshly squeezed lemon juice
- ¼ cup extra-virgin olive oil
- 1 teaspoon minced fresh garlic
- 1 tablespoon chopped fresh parsley
- 2 tablespoons chopped fresh scallions

1. Start by preheating the air fryer to 200°C.
2. Arrange the cauliflower florets in a lightly greased crisper tray.
3. Place the crisper tray in the corresponding position in the air fryer. Select Air Fry and cook the cauliflower florets for about 13 minutes, shaking the crisper tray halfway through the cooking time.
4. Toss the cauliflower florets with the remaining ingredients.
5. Bon appétit!

Bacon Frittata

Prep time: 8 minutes | Cook time: 15 minutes | Serves 4

- 7 eggs
- 4 tablespoons Soured cream
- 1 teaspoon paprika
- flake salt and ground black pepper, to taste
- 2 tablespoons olive oil
- 2 ounces (57 g) bacon, diced
- 1 bell pepper, seeded and diced
- 2 garlic cloves, minced

1. Start by preheating the air fryer to 180°C.
2. Spritz the sides and bottom of the baking pan with nonstick cooking oil.
3. In a mixing bowl, thoroughly combine all the ingredients.
4. Pour the mixture into the prepared baking pan.
5. Place the baking pan in the corresponding position in the air fryer. Select Bake and cook the frittata for approximately 15 minutes, or until a toothpick comes out dry and clean.
6. Bon appétit!

Milk Rabanadas

Prep time: 5 minutes | Cook time: 8 minutes | Serves 2

- 4 slices baguette
- ½ cup full-fat milk
- 4 tablespoons granulated sugar
- 2 eggs, beaten
- ½ teaspoon ground cinnamon
- 2 tablespoons coconut oil

1. Start by preheating the air fryer to 170°C.
2. Toss the bread slices with the remaining ingredients. Transfer to the crisper tray.
3. Place the crisper tray in the corresponding position in the air fryer. Select Air Fry and cook the bread slices for about 4 minutes; turn them over and cook for a further 3 to 4 minutes.
4. Bon appétit!

Brussels Sprout Salad with Apple

Prep time: 10 minutes | Cook time: 10 minutes | Serves 4

- 1 pound (454 g) fresh Brussels sprouts, trimmed
- 1 Vidalia onion, peeled and thinly sliced
- 1 garlic clove, minced
- 1 apple, cored and sliced
- ¼ cup pomegranate arils
- 2 ounces (57 g) goat cheese, crumbled
- 1 tablespoon fresh lemon juice
- ¼ cup extra-virgin olive oil
- 2 tablespoons honey
- 1 tablespoon Dijon mustard

1. Start by preheating the air fryer to 190°C.
2. Arrange the Brussels sprouts in the crisper tray.
3. Place the crisper tray in the corresponding position in the air fryer. Select Air Fry and cook the Brussels sprouts for 10 minutes, shaking the crisper tray halfway through the cooking time.
4. Toss the Brussels sprouts with the remaining ingredients and serve at room temperature. Enjoy!

Buckwheat Cheese Balls

Prep time: 5 minutes | Cook time: 15 minutes | Serves 4

- 1½ cups cooked buckwheat
- 1 cup ground rice
- ½ teaspoon baking powder
- ½ cup grated Parmesan cheese
- 2 eggs, beaten
- 2 tablespoons olive oil
- Sea salt and ground black pepper, to taste

1. Start by preheating the air fryer to 190°C.
2. Mix all the ingredients until everything is well combined. Form the mixture into balls. Transfer to the crisper tray.
3. Place the crisper tray in the corresponding position in the air fryer. Select Air Fry and cook the balls for about 15 minutes or until cooked through, shaking the crisper tray halfway through the cooking time.
4. Bon appétit!

Potato Sinkers

Prep time: 5 minutes | Cook time: 14 minutes | Serves 4

- 1 cup mashed boiled potatoes
- 1 cup plain flour
- ½ teaspoon baking powder
- 2 eggs, beaten
- ½ teaspoon cayenne pepper
- ¼ teaspoon dried dill weed
- ½ teaspoon salt
- ¼ teaspoon ground black pepper

1. Start by preheating the air fryer to 200°C.
2. Mix all the ingredients in a bowl. Shape the mixture into bite-sized balls and place them in a lightly oiled crisper tray.
3. Place the crisper tray in the corresponding position in the air fryer. Select Air Fry and cook the sinkers for about 14 minutes, shaking the crisper tray halfway through the cooking time.
4. Bon appétit!

Appendix 1 Measurement Conversion Chart

Volume Equivalents (Dry)	
US STANDARD	**METRIC (APPROXIMATE)**
1/8 teaspoon	0.5 mL
1/4 teaspoon	1 mL
1/2 teaspoon	2 mL
3/4 teaspoon	4 mL
1 teaspoon	5 mL
1 tablespoon	15 mL
1/4 cup	59 mL
1/2 cup	118 mL
3/4 cup	177 mL
1 cup	235 mL
2 cups	475 mL
3 cups	700 mL
4 cups	1 L

Volume Equivalents (Liquid)		
US STANDARD	**US STANDARD (OUNCES)**	**METRIC (APPROXIMATE)**
2 tablespoons	1 fl.oz.	30 mL
1/4 cup	2 fl.oz.	60 mL
1/2 cup	4 fl.oz.	120 mL
1 cup	8 fl.oz.	240 mL
1 1/2 cup	12 fl.oz.	355 mL
2 cups or 1 pint	16 fl.oz.	475 mL
4 cups or 1 quart	32 fl.oz.	1 L
1 gallon	128 fl.oz.	4 L

Temperatures Equivalents	
FAHRENHEIT(F)	**CELSIUS(C) APPROXIMATE**
225 °F	107 °C
250 °F	120 ° °C
275 °F	135 °C
300 °F	150 °C
325 °F	160 °C
350 °F	180 °C
375 °F	190 °C
400 °F	205 °C
425 °F	220 °C
450 °F	235 °C
475 °F	245 °C
500 °F	260 °C

Weight Equivalents	
US STANDARD	**METRIC (APPROXIMATE)**
1 ounce	28 g
2 ounces	57 g
5 ounces	142 g
10 ounces	284 g
15 ounces	425 g
16 ounces (1 pound)	455 g
1.5 pounds	680 g
2 pounds	907 g

Appendix 2 The Dirty Dozen and Clean Fifteen

The Environmental Working Group (EWG) is a nonprofit, nonpartisan organization dedicated to protecting human health and the environment Its mission is to empower people to live healthier lives in a healthier environment. This organization publishes an annual list of the twelve kinds of produce, in sequence, that have the highest amount of pesticide residue-the Dirty Dozen-as well as a list of the fifteen kinds ofproduce that have the least amount of pesticide residue-the Clean Fifteen.

THE DIRTY DOZEN

The 2016 Dirty Dozen includes the following produce. These are considered among the year's most important produce to buy organic:

Strawberries	Spinach
Apples	Tomatoes
Nectarines	Bell peppers
Peaches	Cherry tomatoes
Celery	Cucumbers
Grapes	Kale/collard greens
Cherries	Hot peppers

The Dirty Dozen list contains two additional itemskale/ collard greens and hot peppers-because they tend to contain trace levels of highly hazardous pesticides.

THE CLEAN FIFTEEN

The least critical to buy organically are the Clean Fifteen list. The following are on the 2016 list:

Avocados	Papayas
Corn	Kiw
Pineapples	Eggplant
Cabbage	Honeydew
Sweet peas	Grapefruit
Onions	Cantaloupe
Asparagus	Cauliflower
Mangos	

Some of the sweet corn sold in the United States are made from genetically engineered (GE) seedstock. Buy organic varieties of these crops to avoid GE produce.

Appendix 3 Index

SALENA L. MELENDEZ

Printed in Great Britain
by Amazon